HIDDEN

H I K E S   I N

WESTERN
WASHINGTON

D0954406

HIDDEN

HIKES IN

WESTERN
WASHINGTON

KAREN SYKES

THE MOUNTAINEERS BOOKS

Published by
The Mountaineers Books
1001 SW Klickitat Way, Suite 201
Seattle, WA 98134

First edition, 2002

Published simultaneously in Great Britain by Cordee, 3a DeMontfort Street, Leicester, England, LE1 7HD

Manufactured in the United States of America

Acquiring Editor: Margaret Sullivan
Project Editor: Christine Ummel Hosler
Copyeditor: Kris Fulsaas
Cover, book design, and layout: Mayumi Thompson
Cartographer: Jim Miller/Fennana Design
Photographs by Karen Sykes, unless otherwise noted

Cover photograph: *Johnson Medra Pass*. Photo by Karen Sykes.
Frontispiece: *The abandoned trail to Chenuis Falls*. Photo by Karen Sykes.

Library of Congress Cataloging-in-Publication Data
Sykes, Karen, 1943–
  Hidden hikes of western Washington / Karen Sykes.— 1st ed.
    p. cm.
Includes bibliographical references (p.) and index.
  ISBN 0-89886-859-9   30 23 77 5 3   4/04
  1. Hiking—Washington (State), Western—Guidebooks. 2.
Trails—Washington (State), Western—Guidebooks. 3. Washington (State),
Western—Guidebooks. I. Title.
  GV199.42.W2 S95 2002
  796.52'2'09797—dc21
                              2001006484

*To the late Harold Engles, with whom I was privileged
to hike, and to Bob Dreisbach, with whom I
continue to hike today*

CONTENTS

US HIGHWAY 2/STEVENS PASS

INTERSTATE 90 WEST OF SNOQUALMIE PASS

INTERSTATE 90 EAST OF SNOQUALMIE PASS

MOUNT RAINIER AND STATE ROUTE 410

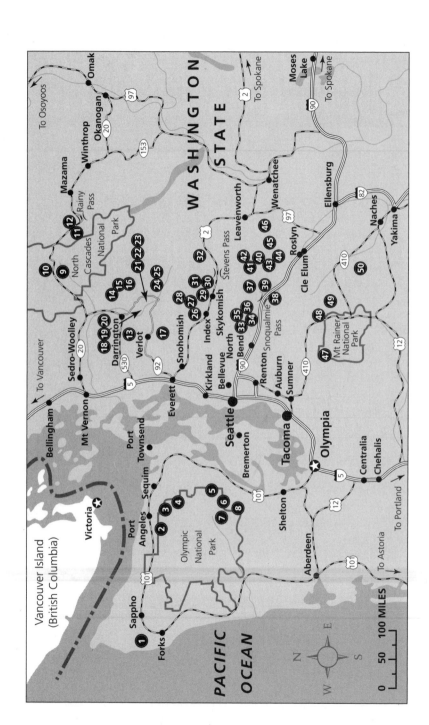

MAP LEGEND

(5)	Interstate Highway	≍	Bridge
(2)	US Highway	▲	Campground, Campsite
(20)	State Route	open A	Picnic Area
6700	Forest Service Road	■	Point of Interest
═══	Interstate Highway	——— -	Wilderness or Park Boundary
═▬═	Paved Road	= = =	Fence or Power Lines
═══	Unpaved Road	(S)	Start of Featured Hike
++++	Railroad	(T)	Alternate Trailhead
----	Featured Route on Trail	≍	Pass
....	Featured Route off Trail	▲	Peak
- - - -	Other Trails	■	Structure
~~	River or Stream	●	Town
~⧘⧘	Falls	✕	Mine
▬▬	Lake		

ACKNOWLEDGMENTS

I could not have completed this work without the help, support, and companionship of many others. Bob Dreisbach not only told me about many abandoned trails but accompanied me on a lot of them. I also give special thanks to Kathy Kelleher, who accompanied me on most of these trails. Her map and compass expertise far surpass mine, and without her I might still be out in the mountains somewhere. Candy Berner, Carl Berner, Randy Busch, Jim Cavin, Sue Edson, Steve Fox, Sally Pfeiffer, and Kathe Stanness were also frequent companions on these brushy journeys. Steve Fox and Randy Busch were tireless when it came to crashing brush and routefinding (some of their "gems" were so difficult that they have been left out of this book). Steve's whimsical sense of humor and Randy's patience with this aging hiker will never be forgotten. I also give special thanks to the personnel of the land management agencies who answered many of my questions and offered a multitude of suggestions.

This book has been enriched by the correspondence, photographs, and memories of two wonderful men who climbed and explored the North Cascades in a time when the Cascades were much wilder than they are today. Special thanks to Keith Markwell and Virgil Peterson for all they shared with me. I thank Joseph Elfelt for the use of his original Forest Service fire plan maps. I also want to acknowledge George Clubine and John Clubine—without their help and expertise with maps, this book would not have seen the light of day. Last but not least, I thank Deborah Easter of The Mountaineers Books for all her help and her faith in me.

Hiking an abandoned trail near Deadwood Lakes

INTRODUCTION

This book is for hikers who enjoy discovering and exploring lesser-known, hidden trails. It is written for the hiker who wants to step off popular trails and experience solitude. It is written mainly for experienced hikers with a sense of adventure who also have route-finding skills. These hikes will also appeal to hikers with an interest in history: many of the trails are historical routes. The hikes in this book cover a variety of trails in the Cascades and the Olympics.

This is not a political book, though there are forces at work regarding hiking in the Northwest that need to be addressed by all hikers. It doesn't take a hiker very long to learn that it is getting more difficult to hike in the mountains. There are simply too many of us, and land management agencies don't have the funds or staffing to maintain existing trails. The combination of budgetary constraints, logging, private ownership of property, lack of trail maintenance (as a result of budget cuts), and too many hikers for too few maintained trails is locking up the wilderness.

However, this book was written in the spirit of optimism rather than despair. We can mourn the trails and those places lost to us, or we can turn in another direction and expand our search. There are many places to be rediscovered, places just waiting for us to show up, trails that for one reason or another have moved to backs of guidebooks but are nonetheless worthy of a second look. Old maps and guidebooks give clues of forgotten trails that can still be explored today.

This is not a climbing guide, though some of the hikes can be extended by some scrambling. Some of these trails go nowhere in particular—you might not get anywhere in the usual sense of the word when it comes to reaching known destinations. What you will get from exploring these trails is the thrill of discovery, a sense of play, the fun of following "clues" and looking for the treasure. The treasure might be a lake, an old mine, a crumbling cabin, or a view few others have seen. Once you step off popular trails, you are entering an intricate web with strands leading out in many directions.

The Little Kachess Trail

WHAT IS A HIDDEN TRAIL?

There are several types of hidden trails—miners' trails, abandoned Forest Service trails, way trails, old roads. A good example of a *miners' trail* is the Neiderprum Trail No. 653 (sometimes referred to as the Lone Tree Pass Trail) in the North Cascades, described here as Hike 13. Most of the trail building done by the Forest Service occurred between 1920 and 1940 when fire lookouts were established. When airplanes took over as a means of spotting fires, many of these trails—and fire lookouts—were *abandoned,* yet some are still passable today. *Way trails,* the third level of Forest Service classification, are rough, steep, and narrow, built to provide quick access to remote areas for firefighting crews. Also in this category are unofficial trails such as routes beaten in by climbers or fishermen.

Old roads such as the CCC Truck Road near North Bend (Hike 33) are also hidden trails. When logging operations are completed, many old roads are abandoned; over time they become overgrown and often make good trails for hikers.

Other hidden trails may appear in guidebooks but are not hiked or maintained on a regular basis. Such trails are in danger of becoming overgrown and therefore can be considered hidden trails. The Bedal Basin Trail No. 705 in the North Cascades (Hike 24) is a good example.

Sign for the Cascade Pass Trail, near Boston Basin
Photo by Steve Fox

HOW TO FIND AND FOLLOW HIDDEN TRAILS

Get off to a good start by doing your homework. Start by getting out maps and guidebooks and studying the area beforehand. Old Forest Service maps are very helpful. You can find (and sometimes copy) such maps at local libraries. Ranger stations may also have old maps that you can look at. Compare the old trails to those shown on the newer Green Trails and USGS maps; many old trails are not shown on new maps.

Look at the maps and interpret the type of terrain you will encounter. Will you be above tree line or in forested river valleys? Will you have to ford streams? Are there permanent snowfields that would require an ice ax? Have a backup hike in case the trail cannot be found or the route becomes hazardous.

When the trail is hard to follow, look for clues such as cut logs, old puncheon (planks or small bridges), or blazes on trees. New blazes are easy to spot because they are obvious, but older blazes are harder to identify. In dense vegetation, look for smooth cuts where brush and branches may have been trimmed away. Sometimes you can tell the difference with your fingers whether a branch has been cut or broken off by natural events. In snow, look for a slight dip that indicates where the trail is.

Try to stay on the trail. Once you are off trail (especially in river valleys), you may face a jungle of devil's club, slide alder, stinging nettles, and heavy brush. If you do lose the route, head for the largest trees, where there may be less underbrush; you may be able to pick up the trail again.

AN ACCOUNT OF A HIDDEN TRAIL

One of the most rewarding hidden trails I explored while researching this book may be regarded as a failure by "peak baggers." My companions and I tried to follow the old Black Creek Trail from the Mountain Loop Highway near Granite Falls, and managed to hike about 2 miles in rough terrain. We never really got anywhere, yet had a wonderful time. We didn't find much of the trail but we found something in ourselves, a part of ourselves that is sometimes lost as we age, and that is the sheer joy of discovery, of seeing something for the first time, the allure of discovering what is at the end of the next switchback. You never know when the magic may happen. You may run into an old-timer out in the middle of nowhere who knows how to get to a lost lake, an old mine, or an unexpected view.

Black Creek doesn't have an obvious trailhead. We read about Black Creek in the out-of-print *Monte Cristo Guide* and were inspired to

A panorama of the North Fork Sauk as taken from Red Pass; Sloan Peak is in the right background.
Photo by Virgil Peterson

explore. Black Creek was the site of a ranger station between 1917 and 1927. The trail, built in 1909, was one of the first major trails constructed by the Forest Service in the Monte Cristo district. Also the site of the Moose Shingle Mill, this trail was maintained for several years as a historical site by the Forest Service.

We found the trail. The interpretive signs are gone, but a trail leads to the mill site. A few timbers and planks remain—bolts, spikes, hinges, and part of a railing still standing, festooned with moss. Tangles of metal gave us no clue as to what function they once served. We also found the one remaining interpretative sign, which reads "SITE OF SHINGLE DRYING SHED," but there was no sign of a shed.

We followed the faint trail as far as we could, but the route soon deteriorated. We found the remains of an old wooden bridge, several

gargantuan stumps from bygone logging eras, and impenetrable walls of brush. There was no point in continuing, so we retreated. We won't go back; that trail is lost forever. We had looked very hard, four of us fanning out in different directions. The forest has taken back the secrets of this trail, but it was exciting to follow the clues and find historical tidbits here and there. We felt our journey was successful.

I hope that this book will inspire you to find your own Black Creek Trail and explore, whether the journey takes you many miles or only a few hundred feet. Once you discover a hidden trail, you will enter a web with many strands. You will find, as we have, that although you have to work harder to discover and follow such old trails, the discovery more than compensates for the work involved. Even the trails that dead-end may nudge another memory and have you poring over old maps and guidebooks, and you may find there are no dead ends, that the trail goes on and does not end as long as you carry the spirit of exploration, curiosity, and discovery within you. When the trail is lost, you simply pick up another strand of the web that may suggest another approach or another destination.

HIDDEN TRAILS—WHAT YOU CAN DO TO SAVE THEM

Many trails that were used in the early 1900s are abandoned or difficult to follow today. A lot of these trails were built by miners, and several of these trails still exist today in the Monte Cristo area, one of The Mountaineers' first areas of exploration. For instance, they camped at Silverton in 1918. Today Silverton is a small town, and the hiking trails from there are closed because they cross private property and the town is peppered with "NO TRESPASSING" signs. A miners' trail that went from Silverton to Marble Pass is omitted from this book because, to avoid trespassing, hikers must either ford the Stillaguamish River or beat brush to get there. You must decide for yourself whether to pursue the old trail. If you can decipher the convoluted route to Marble Pass without trespassing, drowning, or otherwise getting mangled, you will be rewarded with the joy of following historical routes and discovering artifacts.

Some land management agencies are closing roads in an attempt to restore the land to its natural state once logging operations have ceased. In theory this sounds very nice, but in reality it makes access to remote trailheads almost impossible. Perhaps we need to question the policy of closing roads and trails and limiting access for experienced hikers with cross-country hiking skills who would like to explore these trails before they are gone.

Several trails have been left out of this book at the request of the Forest Service because the terrain is too challenging, there is limited parking, or for environmental concerns. For example, I have been asked not to include the Keep Kool Trail, which the Forest Service closed to revegetate meadows that have suffered overuse, because the parking is limited, and because of perceived hazards on the route. In its place a new trail has been built; the route to Yellow Aster Butte now begins from the Tomyhoi Lake Trailhead. The new trail is excellent; it is a pleasure to hike and the scenery is profound. There is just one small problem. On a recent Saturday, there were thirty-five cars at the trailhead and hundreds of people on the trail. It was no longer a wilderness experience. If hikers think they are going to find solitude on this trail, they are in for disappointment.

However, I still believe it is in the best interests of all of us to work with the land management agencies rather than against them. I also believe that many hikers don't know about these changes and

An abandoned logging truck, discovered off a trail near North Bend
Photo by Steve Fox

need to be informed so they can make their own decisions and decide whether to get involved or become activists. It is up to each and every one of us to decide how far we want to go to change this trend of closing trails and herding hikers onto a dwindling number of trails that are regularly maintained.

Today those who wish to work on trails are well advised to join an organization such as Washington Trails Association or Volunteers of Washington. Such groups work in conjunction with the Forest Service and have done an excellent job. The list of trail maintenance opportunities is growing exponentially. If not for such organizations, more trails would have been lost by now.

There is also a growing underground movement of hikers who are quietly taking some lost trails back and working on their own to clear brush and open old routes. You may be tempted to join them when you have had the pleasure of following old trails and discovering cut logs, old blazes, and puncheon. However, there are laws and regulations governing such activities (especially in wilderness areas), so be sure you are not breaking any laws.

HIKING BASICS

You need to be in good physical condition for most of these trails. Although most of these hikes are not backpacking trips or high-mileage routes, occasionally you have to fight brush, negotiate blowdowns, use your routefinding skills, scramble over boulders, and ford streams; progress may sometimes be slow. Establish a sensible turnaround time and allow for error. Always tell someone where you are going and when you will return. Do not rely on a cell phone to get you out of trouble.

Take a Mountaineering Oriented First Aid course (known as MOFA), in which you learn how to stabilize an injured person until rescue can take place; the focus is on accidents that can result from being in the mountains. Some hikers carry an accident report form with them with the telephone numbers for appropriate authorities.

Regulations and Permits

Rules, regulations, and fees are constantly changing. Before you set out, call the land management agency (see Appendix A at the back of this book) for recent trail and road conditions. Here are some general regulations to be aware of: Motorized vehicles are not allowed in national parks or in designated wilderness areas. Because hunting and fishing regulations vary greatly, hikers who are interested in hunting or fishing should contact the state Department of Fish and Wildlife. In general, a fishing license is required in national forests but not in the national parks. Fires are prohibited above 3,500 feet in wilderness areas, but for reduced impact it is always best to rely on a backpacking stove rather than a campfire. Backcountry permits are required for all overnight camping in national parks; obtain them at ranger stations or park entry roads. A Northwest Forest Pass is now required by the Forest Service to park at most national forest trailheads; they also can be purchased at ranger stations as well as outdoor equipment outlets. In 2002, a one-day Northwest Forest Pass cost $5 and an annual pass cost $30.

Wilderness Ethics On or Off the Trail

It is imperative that all hikers practice minimum impact when in the backcountry. Special considerations must be taken once you step off trail so you leave no damage to the environment. When you walk off trail, avoid stepping on plants if you can; step on rocks if possible. Do not establish cairns or flag routes when off trail; it is no longer considered politically correct to flag a route—if you do flag a route, be sure to take the flagging down on your return.

When nature calls, use backcountry toilets where they are provided. Where they are not, find a site where others are unlikely to visit; always choose a site more than 200 feet away from water. Bury your waste at least 6 inches with the use of a trowel or even an ice ax. If there is no backcountry toilet, pack out soiled toilet paper. Some hikers even pack out their human waste.

When camping, use established campsites wherever possible or camp on hard surfaces such as dirt, rock, or snow. Do not camp on dry grass or meadows, shrubs, succulent plants, or heather. Use a hiking stove

Chocolate lily

whenever possible; where fires are permitted and safe, keep them small, build them only in existing fire rings, and use only dead and down wood from outside the camp area. After you break camp, make sure you leave no trace. Pack out what you pack in.

Water Treatment

All water in the backcountry must be treated. *Giardia lamblia* (a waterborne protozoan) inhabits not only water in lakes and streams, but also can be found in water from snowmelt. Do not assume that any water is safe. Iodine or chlorine tablets are effective in treating water for bacteria and viruses but not protozoa, and some people don't like the taste. Some hikers use water filters, which filter out protozoa but not all bacteria and viruses; filters can be expensive and time-consuming—I've seen them break down on extended trips. You can filter water and then treat it with iodine or chlorine to be sure you've killed all pathogens, but boiling remains the most effective means of treating water, though there is some controversy about how long water should be boiled. Bringing water to a boil is sufficient to kill bacteria, viruses, and protozoa, but if it makes you feel better, let it boil a couple of minutes.

The Ten Essentials

Make sure you have all the Ten Essentials in your pack, even for a day hike on a warm summer day. If you have the Ten Essentials, you should be able to survive a bivouac—not necessarily in comfort, but you will survive.

1. Map
2. Compass
3. Headlamp (with spare batteries and bulbs)
4. Extra food
5. Extra clothing
6. Sunglasses
7. First-aid kit
8. Pocketknife
9. Matches (in waterproof container) or a lighter
10. Fire starter

Some hikers carry more, depending on the intensity of their activity. Other items may include an emergency shelter or blanket, trash bags (they can serve a multitude of purposes, including emergency shelter), water filter, and a small insulated pad. Ice axes should be taken on hikes where snow will be encountered and/or on trails where they come in handy for balance. Some hikers prefer collapsible ski poles for this purpose.

SAFETY CONCERNS

Hazards are an innate characteristic of mountainous terrain. It is helpful to recognize potential hazards before you set out and be prepared to deal with them. For example, if you come across mines in your explorations, never enter them, as many mines contain winzes (vertical mine shafts) of unknown depth that are sometimes flooded.

Knowledge of hazards is crucial to being in the backcountry. You need to know when it is safe to cross a stream and when it is not. You need to know about avalanches and how to avoid them. You need to have an idea of what weather conditions to expect. You need to know what sort of wildlife you might encounter. You need to be prepared to survive a bivouac if you have to.

Stream Crossings

Generally, if the water is deep and swift and above the knees, due consideration should be given whether to proceed or turn around. When in doubt, turn around. If you do decide to cross, keep in mind that it is generally easier and often safer to cross a stream in the morning; afternoon sun can create runoff in late spring. During a heavy rain, water levels can also rise.

Look about for a safe place to wade across. In general look for a wide, shallow place to cross if you must ford. The narrow sections of the river might look tempting but these can be deceptive with swift water and strong currents. Ford early in the morning when streams tend to be low (snowmelt on warm days can cause stream levels to rise). Algae grow on rocks and gravel in streams, which makes them slippery—another good reason to cross where the stream is wide and shallow. Some hikers carry an extra pair of tennis shoes or boat shoes for the sole purpose of fording streams—it's never a good idea to cross barefoot because rocks are slippery underwater.

Don't cross in haste; take the time to walk up and down the stream to see if there is a safer place to cross. Read the water: waves are created by the flow of the water as it pours over submerged objects, which may give a clue to what lies beneath. A downstream V may indicate a deep channel, whereas a V pointing upstream is probably caused by water flowing around a submerged snag or boulder. Be suspicious of humps in the water that indicate a hole in the riverbed just above it (these are also found downstream of boulders). Unfasten your pack straps when

Hikers negotiate a stream crossing in the central Cascades.

you ford because the weight of your fastened pack can hold you under the water if you slip. Better to lose the pack than your life.

If conditions permit, walk across a stream on logs—you may be able to find a logjam up- or downstream from the trail. If possible, build a simple footbridge out of logs and fallen timber. If you are not comfortable walking upright across logs above streams, you may be able to scoot across on your bottom.

Avalanches

Although hikers may encounter permanent snowfields on some of the trails and routes in this book, avalanche hazards and terrain are not covered in any detail here. However, avalanches do occur year-round in our mountains, even in spring and summer. A small avalanche can do a lot of damage if you are in the wrong place at the wrong time. I know of two specific instances in which small, shallow avalanches injured hikers in the Snoqualmie Pass area. One of these occurred on Mailbox Peak near North Bend, a peak that should be taken more seriously when there is significant snow. In general, stay in trees as much as possible when traveling on snow, because open slopes are more prone to slide. Take a course on avalanche awareness before you go hiking, scrambling, or backpacking where significant snow may be a consideration.

Weather

Weather can change quickly in the Northwest. When we were on the eastern side of the Cascades once, we were holed up by a snowstorm for three days—in July. Always get a weather forecast before you set out on your hike. In addition to local newscasts and newspapers, there are weather-related websites you can browse via the Internet. One of the best I've found is *www.wowweather.com*. This forecast is reliable and, in addition to weather, it suggests destinations appropriate for the forecast and information on road and trail closures.

Remember that the Ten Essentials include extra food and clothing! Even light rain or drizzle can dampen not only your spirits but your gear as well. Be prepared with the best raingear you can afford, and make sure that the seams of your raingear, boots, and tent are sealed.

Hypothermia and Heat Exhaustion

Hypothermia occurs when your body reaches too low a temperature to generate its own heat. This is caused by a variety of conditions, but usually occurs when you are wet and/or chilled. Commonly this is due to a combination of cold temperature, rain, and wind, though you can also get wet from sweat in even moderate temperatures. If you are wet and chilled, change into dry clothing as soon as possible. You risk hypothermia if you are not adequately prepared; wear clothing that protects you from not only rain but wind.

Heat exhaustion is just what it implies—overexertion in heat. During hot weather, drink plenty of water and dress lightly. Stop and rest when you get too hot—it helps to be in good condition as well. On backpacking trips, travel in the cooler parts of the day. Be sure to take heat exhaustion seriously, because it can progress to heat stroke and become life threatening.

Lions and Tigers and Bears, Oh My!

In the Northwest, this refrain would more likely be "snakes and bugs and bears." On the east side of the Cascades, you may encounter rattlesnakes in the spring and summer as they sun themselves on rocks; we almost stepped on one near Icicle Ridge. Keep on the lookout for snakes and avoid them; they usually will slither away if given the chance. They can be found sunning themselves on rocks or traveling through tall grasses. You may hear one before you see one. The

Mountaineering Oriented First Aid course, which is offered several times a year, covers treatment of snakebite in detail.

Watch for ticks, especially on the eastern side of the Cascades in the spring; they also have been found at Ross Lake and Deception Pass. Examine your clothing, gear, and self when you get back to the car, especially if you have been thrashing in brush or grass. Tick-transmitted Lyme disease is not as prevalent in the Northwest as in other sections of the country, but it has become a growing threat.

Yellowjackets and hornets can create a lot of grief for hikers in late summer and early fall. If you are allergic to them, carry a bee-sting kit; you should also be the first person on the trail in your party. Hornets and such are more apt to attack the second or third person in line. Mosquitoes and biting flies are most commonly the hiker's scourge. Some people are more prone to being bitten than others. Move to higher ground where breezes may keep them at bay. For all insect pests, wear insect repellent or protective clothing—or both. However, insect repellent is not very effective against ticks.

Encounters with black bears are becoming more common in our mountains. Some sections of the backcountry may be closed off if there have been significant problems. Avoid areas where bears are known to be if you can. If you are in bear country, stay out of their personal space and don't surprise them. If you see or hear bears, make noise on the trail and in your tent. Black bears can climb, and they will attack to protect their young. If you see cubs on or near the trail, the mother is probably nearby too. Move away. Brown bears—grizzlies—are more likely to attack (but you are more likely to encounter a black bear in our mountains); if you meet one face to face, do not run because it may trigger pursuit. In general I have found that bears are more frightened of us than we are of them, but don't take unnecessary risks.

Because bears have an acute sense of smell, your camp kitchen area should be at least 100 yards downwind from your tent. Use no soap or detergent when washing cookware, and burn (or triple-bag) everything (meat or fish residue and used feminine hygiene articles) that might attract a bear. It helps to package food in containers with tight lids or in sealed plastic bags. Special unbreakable plastic bear-resistant food containers are effective for storing food, and are now required in some areas. Bears are not the only problem. Rodents will gnaw their way

A hiker changes into dry socks, a good step toward avoiding hypothermia.

through plastic bags, packs, even tents. Hang your food (or pack) by a cord from a tree or suspended from a pole. To be effective, it must be farther from the trunk of the tree and higher that a bear can reach from the ground (12 feet from the ground and 4 feet from the tree trunk). Some camping spots provide "bear wire" for this purpose. Keep in mind that mice can walk the wire and drop down to the food source; raccoons can go out on a branch and pull the food by its line. Raccoons are extremely persistent on the shores of the Pacific (Sand Point and Cape Alava are popular hangouts for these furry thugs), and at dusk you are apt to see their shining eyes around your campfire as you dine. If you can't hang the food or you don't have appropriate containers, divide the food among your party so that if one pack or cache is broken into, your party won't go hungry.

Cougar encounters have become more common as their habitat has shrunk. Children and small adults are the most at risk from cougar attacks. However, they are more apt to see you than you are to see them. If you are alone in the backcountry and encounter one, do not run because they may take up the chase. Try to make yourself appear as large as possible, stand your ground, and do not turn your back on the cougar.

Getting Lost or Having to Bivouac

Though the backcountry is a beautiful place to be, things can go wrong. Weather can change. People can get hurt—even experienced hikers are not immune to accidents, which can happen anywhere. And getting lost is a real consideration when routefinding on trails such as the ones in this book.

Hopefully none of this will ever happen to you, but you should be prepared just the same. Have enough food, clothing, and bivouac equipment to get through that period of time in which you are lost (see The Ten Essentials section in Hiking Basics, above). Bivouacs are often the end result of bad weather or judgment, injury, or getting lost, though a bivouac doesn't necessarily mean you're lost—you're just not able to return to the trailhead in one day as planned. Many experienced hikers and scramblers I know have had to bivouac for one reason or another, usually because they did not allow enough time for their return trip. Also, "stuff happens." Expect the unexpected. Sometimes hikers overestimate their abilities, travel without a map, or don't get an update on trail conditions before setting out. Others may not pay enough attention to the route and lose it on their way back. I always make it a point to turn around several times and look where I have come from so I recognize the terrain on the way back, especially in an area I am not familiar with or off trail. Anyone who is tired is capable of missing a junction or getting on a game trail at the end of a switchback. Worse, some hikers tend to keep going when they shouldn't—they are too tired, the weather is getting worse, or they are running out of daylight.

If you are lost, stop and try to determine your whereabouts. If that fails, backtrack to your last known location if it is close and see if that helps. If your last known point is too far away, then proceed with caution and look for landmarks but be prepared to bivouac. Although some hikers enjoy solo hikes, it is safer to travel with at least one other person. If in a group, try to keep everyone together and establish a rear guard. If you are alone, try to find your location with the map and plan a route. If you have become separated from others, you can mark your location with a cairn, then scout. Just be sure to return to your marked position. Get prepared to bivouac before it gets dark—find water, shelter, and firewood. If you don't reconnect with your party by morning or if you are not found by then, you can attempt to hike out to a prominent feature such as a ridge, highway, or stream. If the terrain is too challenging, stay put and wait to be found.

HOW TO USE THIS BOOK

The hikes described in this book range from easy to difficult in terms of physical exertion required, but many of them require routefinding skills and a high tolerance for brushy, unmaintained trails. Beginning hikers are advised to hike on maintained trails described in other hiking guidebooks because hikers need to acquire trail experience before exploring these hidden trails. Many of the trails included here are easier trails that most experienced hikers can hike without difficulty. Several of these trails are in good condition with only minor blowdowns, but certain skills are strongly recommended nonetheless.

You should have the ability to use a map and compass, but you also need what some loosely call "mountain sense." This is something that is acquired over time, from years of hiking in all kinds of conditions and terrain. You need to know what works for you in terms of gear and clothing and be able to adjust them accordingly as conditions change.

If you are new to hiking, you can take a scrambling course or a course in navigation—such courses are very helpful for exploring some of the more challenging trails offered in this book, such as the route to the Double Eagle Mine near Silverton in the North Cascades (Hike 20) or the forgotten segment of the Nason Ridge Trail near Stevens Pass (Hike 32). If you are new to the Northwest, acquaint yourself with the

A raccoon, a cute but unwelcome guest

area on easier hikes. You don't need to be a mountain climber to explore these trails, but you may be crawling, scrambling, ducking under trees, and negotiating through tangles of brush and blowdowns—and you will get dirty. Progress may be slow. It may take half a day to hike 2 miles, but there are rewards for those who are inspired to pursue adventure and exploration.

At the beginning of each hike, an information summary lists distance, difficulty rating, type of trail, elevations, season, maps, contact information, and cautions. **Distance** is given in miles, usually round trip; sometimes these are approximations. **Difficulty** ratings are a bit different in this book because *all* of the trails require experience, so this category doesn't include *Easy; Moderate, Challenging,* and *Extremely challenging* give a general indication of how long the hike is, how much elevation gain there is, how tricky the routefinding can be, and how much physical exertion is required. **Type of trail** describes not only the trail's origins—way trail established by firefighting crews, climbers, or fishermen; miners' trail; Forest Service or Park Service trail; old road; or some combination—but also indicates the level of maintenance it's had: maintained, occasionally maintained, or abandoned (unmaintained). This entry also gives an idea of how difficult the hike might be. **Starting point**, **High point**, and **Elevation gain** are all given in feet—again, giving clues to how strenuous the physical exertion will be. The **Hikable** entry indicates the best times of year to do the hike. **Maps** listed are usually Green Trails, Custom Correct, or USGS maps. The **Information** entry lists the land management agency (or agencies) to contact and their phone number(s). **Cautions** tell you what hazards or impediments you can expect to encounter.

After the information summary, an overview describes the attractions of the hike and what type of hiker the route is recommended for. Following that are directions to the trailhead, then a description of the hike itself. Because these hikes are on less-maintained trails and require at least some routefinding, trail descriptions may not be as detailed as those found in more traditional hiking guides. Landmarks such as trail junctions, bridges, and established backcountry campsites may not exist on some of these hikes, so incremental mileage points may be more approximate in this book.

In addition to the text, most of the hikes include a map and a photograph. On the maps, the hike I've described appears as a dark dashed line where it's on a trail, and as a dotted line where it goes off-trail. Other trails in the area appear as light dashed lines. However, the maps in this book are intended only as an overview of the hike's location; hikers should obtain and use the recommended Green Trails or USGS map to navigate.

A NOTE ABOUT SAFETY

Safety is an important concern in all outdoor activities. No guidebook can alert you to every hazard or anticipate the limitations of every reader. Therefore, the descriptions of roads, trails, routes, and natural features in this book are not representations that a particular place or excursion will be safe for your party. When you follow any of the routes described in this book, you assume responsibility for your own safety. Under normal conditions, such excursions require the usual attention to traffic, road and trail conditions, weather, terrain, the capabilities of your party, and other factors. Keeping informed on current conditions and exercising common sense are the keys to a safe, enjoyable outing.

The Mountaineers Books

Old-growth forest

THE OLYMPICS

1 ALLENS BAY TRAIL

Distance: 4.8 miles round trip to Norwegian Memorial
Difficulty: Moderate
Type of trail: Abandoned
Starting point: Sea level
High point: 120 feet
Elevation gain: 120 feet
Hikable: Year-round
Maps: Custom Correct North Olympic Coast; Green Trails
  No. 1305 Ozette
Information: Olympic National Park Wilderness
  Information Center, 360-565-3100
Cautions: Brush, deteriorating boardwalks and bridges;
  requires either a boat or a long approach

Hikers with an interest in history will find the Lake Ozette area full of it, particularly abandoned trails such as the Allens Bay Trail to the Norwegian Memorial. The Makah Indians knew the lake as *Ka'houk*, and it was sometimes shown on old maps as Lake of the Sun. Both the lake and the wilderness coast a few miles to the west are part of Olympic National Park. Lake Ozette is good for fishing largemouth bass, cutthroat trout, yellow perch, and squawfish in addition to steelhead and silver salmon. Though this trail is short and has little elevation gain, there are hazardous sections near Allens Bay, and a long backpacking trip on the coast is needed if you don't have a boat.

Lake Ozette is one of the largest natural lakes in Washington, with several islands. The 22-acre Tivoli Island, located in the southern section of the lake, was named by Scandinavian immigrants. E. F. "Tivoli" Neilson was an early settler who homesteaded on the island and planned to make it into a showplace similar to the Tivoli Garden in Denmark. He planted Norwegian chestnuts, maples, beeches, and cork trees and even brought in frogs to enhance the garden. Today some of the trees still stand, but other signs of habitation are gone. Garden Island was also named by Scandinavian settlers. Camping is permitted on Tivoli Island (a backcountry permit is required). Ericksons Bay was named for Norwegian pioneer Ole Erickson, who built a cabin there in 1890. Allens Bay was first homesteaded in 1893 by a family named Peterson. They built a two-room cabin from a single cedar log, and one of the rooms served as a grocery store. A post office was

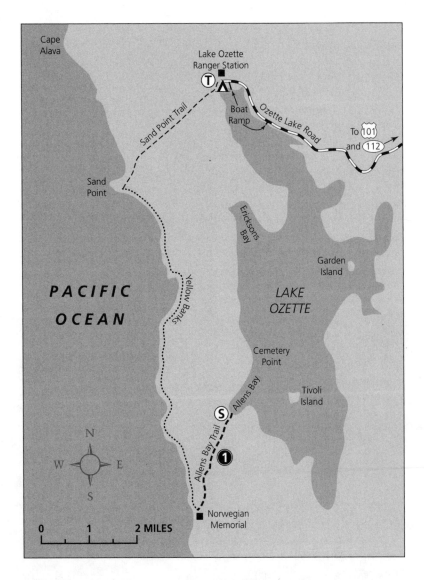

established there in 1894, and the mail was delivered once a week. The bay was named for the second homesteader on Tivoli Island, A. C. Allen, who served as postmaster. Allen apparently drowned while delivering mail to settlers; his boat capsized in a sudden storm on Lake Ozette. At one time there were about 130 homesteads around the lake. Travel was by horse, foot, or boats and canoes. The Norwegian

Memorial, on the Pacific Coast west of Allens Bay, commemorates the shipwreck of eighteen Norwegian sailors who lost their lives in 1903 when their ship, *Prince Arthur of Norway,* was wrecked on the coast. Only two sailors survived.

During World War II, this area was patrolled by the Coast Guard, fueled by fears of invasion or sabotage. The Beach Patrol, as it was known, was established to report suspicious activities along the coastline. There were four Beach Patrol units stationed along the Washington coast. Ozette Beach was one of them; it may have been the most challenging, with 12 miles of coastline patrolled each day. Base Camp at Lake Ozette, situated at the north end of the lake, was a luxury compared to camps on the beach. The Coast Guardsmen hacked out trails between Lake Ozette and the ocean. Passage from inland wooded areas to the beaches was almost impossible. The terrain was swampy, so split logs were used to make corduroy trails (raised trails of wooden planks). Enough trails—18 miles—were built to set up five patrol posts along the beach.

Allens Bay

The Coast Guard required men to travel in pairs on their patrols. The men were armed and reported in from telephone boxes placed at specific intervals along the beaches. In areas especially vulnerable to sabotage, vigils were conducted around the clock. In addition to climbing and descending rocky headlands, patrolmen faced the challenge of the rain forest with its accompanying drizzle, fog, and cool temperatures. Conditions on the beach were primitive—initially the men cooked over an open fire. Later the patrols carried in tents and a woodstove to make life on the beach a little more bearable. Small boats were brought in by the Navy to be used on the lake, which cut down on the time spent hiking to the beach.

Eventually more men were needed for sea duty, and as the fears of invasion diminished, a reduction in Beach Patrol was ordered; by 1944 only the West Coast had an active patrol. Few traces of the Beach Patrol remain today other than a few telephone insulators that can still be seen on trees and traces of their trails. The Allens Bay Trail has been abandoned for some time.

To get to Lake Ozette, drive US 101 west from Port Angeles. Between mileposts 242 and 243, go right on State Route 112 past Sekiu, turn left on Ozette Lake Road, and drive to the road end and ranger station (elevation 36 feet). There are restrooms and a campground. Boating and fishing regulations are posted at the ranger station. Reservations are required on the wilderness coast from Point of the Arches to Yellow Banks, from May 1 through September. Rules, fees, permits, and regulations are subject to change; call the Olympic National Park Wilderness Information Center before you go.

From the Lake Ozette Ranger Station, there are two ways to get to the Allens Bay Trail: you can boat in to Allens Bay, 7 miles south of the Lake Ozette Ranger Station, or you can make a long hike from the Lake Ozette Ranger Station to the coast at Sand Point and south on the coast to the Norwegian Memorial, hiking the Allens Bay Trail in reverse of what's described here. For this trail description, boat down to Allens Bay.

It is a rough 2.4-mile trail from Allens Bay to the Norwegian Memorial. The trailhead at Allens Bay is not marked; when you get to the bay, look for the opening in the reeds where you can pull your boat up on the beach. Primitive campsites are found a short distance from the lakeshore and the start of the unsigned trail. The most dangerous section of the trail is located a short distance from Allens Bay—a decaying bridge with missing planks. The planks of the bridge that are still in place slant downhill and footing is precarious. Someone has cut back the brush from time to time, but there are slippery boardwalks, boggy sections, and a few large trees down over the trail that have to be climbed over. As the trail approaches the ocean, it improves and can quite easily be followed through brush and salal as it makes a gradual descent to the Norwegian Memorial. The beach trailhead is marked with a sign reading "ROUTE NOT MAINTAINED."

If you opt to hike along the coast to the Norwegian Memorial you'll find it's 12 miles one way from the ranger station to Allens Bay. From the Lake Ozette Ranger Station, hike 3 miles on the Sand Point Trail to the coast. From Sand Point, follow the coast south past Yellow Banks, which can only be hiked during low tides (be sure to carry a tide table and the map); it is 7.2 miles from Sand Point to the Norwegian Memorial. Then follow the Allens Bay Trail description in reverse, from the Norwegian Memorial to Allens Bay.

2 LITTLE RIVER TRAIL

Distance: 15.8 miles round trip
Difficulty: Challenging
Type of trail: Occasionally maintained NPS trail
Starting point: 990 feet
High point: 5,125 feet
Elevation gain: 4,135 feet
Hikable: Spring, summer, fall (lower section in winter)
Map: Custom Correct Hurricane Ridge
Information: Olympic National Park Wilderness
    Information Center, 360-565-3100
Cautions: Blowdowns, brush, stream crossings, avalanche
    danger in spring

The Little River Trail is a strenuous 8-mile trail in Olympic National Park (backcountry permit required) that climbs to Hurricane Ridge. Hikers and backpackers who want solitude and scenery will find them here. The trail doesn't seem to get much use, nor is it prominently featured in hiking guides. The first 5 miles of the trail can often be hiked in the winter, with many suitable places to camp along the way. There are also many stream crossings, some of them on logs or unbridged. Conditions change from year to year and some of the bridges may be missing. One bridge has been knocked askew and can still be used with caution, though it lies at a wicked slant. In summer it

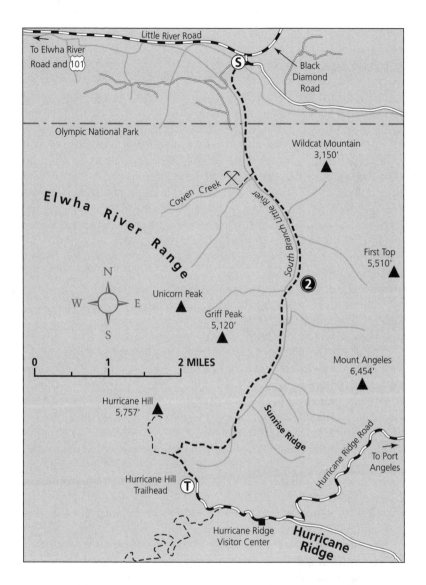

is not difficult to ford the Little River here. If you plan to hike the entire trail one way, save the hike for later in the season when stream levels are low and Hurricane Ridge is free of snow. For a one-way hike you'll need to have a second vehicle for a shuttle or arrange to have someone pick you up. Most one-way hikers prefer to hike from top to bottom, beginning at Hurricane Ridge and descending the Little River

Trail, because it is easier to lose the more than 4,100 feet in elevation change than gain it. However, the trail is described here from bottom to top because a good portion of it is hikable in winter when the upper sections are snow-covered; in summer it does make sense to hike from top to bottom. For overnight hikes, a wilderness camping permit is required, which can be obtained at the Olympic National Park Wilderness Information Center in Port Angeles.

To reach the Little River Trailhead, from Port Angeles drive west on US 101 for 8.5 miles and turn left on the Elwha River Road. At less than 0.5 mile, look for the Little River Road branching off to the left, and turn onto it. Drive east a couple of miles, and a short distance past a junction with the Black Diamond Road, look for the trailhead on the right and a small parking area on the left. To start up on Hurricane Ridge and hike down to the Little River, drive to the upper trailhead. Take the Hurricane Ridge Road from Port Angeles, which climbs through foothills to Heart of the Hills entrance station and a campground, continuing to Hurricane Ridge at 17.5 miles. From the Hurricane Ridge Visitor Center, continue west to parking for the Hurricane Hill Trailhead. Hike the wide, easy trail about 0.4 mile to the signed junction with the Little River Trail on the right.

From the Little River Trailhead, the trail follows the south branch of the Little River, a tributary of the Elwha River, beginning in second-growth forest. The trail is bordered by Mount Angeles, Wildcat Mountain, and the Elwha River Range. At 1.3 miles the trail enters Olympic National Park; beyond the park boundary the forest consists of old-growth fir, cedar, and hemlock. Rocky cliffs loom over the trail as it parallels the river. There are three of these giant, fern-covered basalt boulders noteworthy enough to have been given the name Gnome Rocks. Beyond the first Gnome, the trail makes the first of ten river and stream crossings (not all shown on map, previous page), any of which have the potential to be a challenge depending on the time of year and conditions.

At the second crossing, at about 1.7 miles at Cowen Creek, there is a junction with a path to the right that leads to an abandoned mine and is hard to follow; stay left. After the next two stream crossings, the trail passes the other two Gnome Rocks before crossing the river again, adding up to five crossings in less than a mile. The sixth crossing is especially scenic, the river spanned by a log across a deep pool. The broad foot log is festooned with moss and small flowering plants.

Beyond the seventh crossing at about 3.8 miles, the trail begins to

Crossing the Little River

climb and the character of the forest changes accordingly. Western hemlock and silver fir replace the Douglas firs found at lower elevations. Expect blowdowns once you have made this crossing. Several trees have fallen over the trail, but hikers have created detours around the worst of these.

The last three crossings are easy because the stream is shallow. Look for an old campsite near the eighth crossing at about 6 miles. The country opens up as the trail climbs with ever-expanding views across a small valley to meadowlands and mountain slopes dotted with evergreens and shrubbery. In early August the meadows are bright with flowers—valerian, magenta paintbrush, tiger lilies, yarrow, cow parsley, arnica, larkspur, and penstemon. The grade steepens as the trail switchbacks through meadows and stands of subalpine fir with some blowdowns continuing all the way to the Hurricane Hill trail junction at 7.9 miles. At the junction, to the left it is 0.4 mile to the parking lot for the Hurricane Hill Trailhead; to the right it is 1 mile to the summit of Hurricane Hill (5,757 feet), where a fire lookout once stood.

3 COX VALLEY TRAIL

Distance: 3.6 miles round trip
Difficulty: Moderate
Type of trail: Occasionally maintained NPS trail
Starting point: 4,870 feet
Low point: 3,600 feet
Elevation loss: 1,270 feet
Hikable: Summer, fall
Maps: Green Trails No. 135 Mt. Angeles; Custom Correct
  Hurricane Ridge
Information: Olympic National Park Wilderness
  Information Center, 360-565-3100
Cautions: Blowdowns

This is an old trail (once known as the Morse Creek Trail) named for
an early settler, A. E. Cox. Cox and a friend built homesteads near
each other and constructed a trail that ascended Morse Creek; Cox
Valley is the upper part of the Morse Creek valley. Cox used the trail
when he worked as a county game warden. The trail once extended

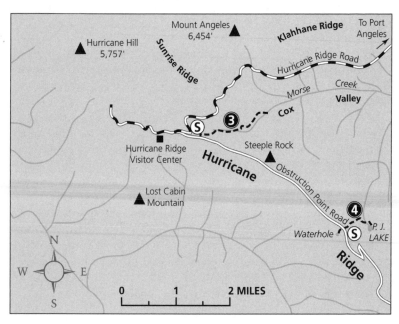

the length of the Morse Creek valley to the boundary of Olympic National Park, but construction of the Hurricane Ridge Road has made the trail obsolete, and it is seldom used today. Though the Cox Valley Trail is not steep, the terrain is not always easy—you may be struggling through blowdowns or hiking through through boggy meadows where the trail has disappeared. Lack of regular maintenance, as well as lack of public awareness and interest, are causing this trail to fall into obsolescence. Also, most hikers prefer to walk downhill on the way out after climbing "up" to something, and the Cox Valley Trail does the opposite, descending more than 1,200 feet and fading out in a meadow, so the elevation is gained on the way out. Most hikers want to get to the high country as soon as they can, and farther up the road is Grand Ridge, where they need only step out of their car to get good views.

So why hike this trail at all? Because it is lonesome, the meadows are beautiful, and the chances of encountering wildlife are greater than on popular trails crowded with other hikers. In late September the meadows are wearing their fall colors but a few flowers are still blooming, hinting of their summer brilliance. As you descend into the lower meadows, to the northeast there are good views of Burnt Mountain, so named because a forest fire swept over the region in the late 1890s. When the trail drops from the access road, hikers may find it interesting and a bit disconcerting to watch the string of cars climbing the hill to Hurricane Ridge on the other side of the valley. Drop a few feet more and the cars are gone, the valley quiet once more.

From Port Angeles take the Hurricane Ridge Road, which climbs through foothills to Heart of the Hills entrance station and a campground. In about 17 miles, just before the Hurricane Ridge Visitor Center, make an extremely sharp left-hand turn onto the Obstruction Point Road, which heads downhill. (If you end up at the Hurricane Ridge Visitor Center, you missed the Obstruction Point Road.) The signed Cox Valley Trailhead is 0.5 mile east on the Obstruction Point Road, on the left. Just beyond the trailhead there is a small parking area with enough room for two cars. There are no facilities.

Though a hiking guide states that the trail is abandoned, the first 0.5 mile of the trail is presently maintained as it switchbacks steeply down to the first meadow. Rangers we met told of "100 trees" across the trail, and we did encounter several of them where the trail crew had stopped their work. Several blowdowns interrupt the flow of the trail as it goes gently downhill through a mixture of meadows and forests. Just beyond a campsite at about 0.8 mile (a mileage marker can be found on a tree

A hiker negotiates a blowdown.

here), cross the headwaters of Morse Creek, here a small stream, twice.

Where the route is vague, a few strategic ribbons have been placed—please do not remove them. They do no harm here, and some hikers may need them to follow what is left of the trail. They are placed only where the tread has virtually vanished. However, do not add flagging because it creates confusion and is unsightly.

Beyond the campsite, the trail descends to cross the stream again. This crossing is made more interesting by a blowdown that must be crawled over as soon as you climb out of the creek. The trail enters another meadow with a thick wall of slide alder to the left; then the trail continues downhill. To the northeast are views of Klahhane Ridge and straight ahead is another view of Burnt Mountain. *Klahhane* is a Chinook term that translates to "good times in the mountains" or "outside."

The trail ends in another large meadow at 1.8 miles. This is probably as far as you will want to hike, though guidebooks suggest that experienced hikers can explore further by following occasional ribbons. There are rumors of the remains of a cabin in one of the meadows and a stand of Engelmann spruce along another forgotten trail.

4 P. J. LAKE TRAIL

Distance: 1.8 miles round trip
Difficulty: Moderate
Type of trail: Maintained NPS trail
Starting point: 5,020 feet
Low point: 4,400 feet
Elevation loss: 620 feet
Hikable: Summer, fall
Map: Custom Correct Hurricane Ridge
Information: Olympic National Park Wilderness
    Information Center, 360-565-3100
Cautions: None
See Hike 3 for map

The P. J. Lake Trail was created by fishermen, and the name evolved over the years as they hiked the steep trail down to the favorite lake of P. J. Williams, an early resident of Port Angeles who was an outdoor enthusiast and loved to fish. The lake is situated at the base of Eagle Point, which is 6,247 feet high. The trailhead is at "Waterhole Camp," site of a small spring, the only springwater available along the crest of

P. J. Lake

Hurricane Ridge. Waterhole Camp was a popular picnic area in the 1960s; for a few years there was a ski hut located here that skiers could reserve by means of a lottery system. Today nothing remains other than the parking area and the trailhead. The P. J. Lake Trail, maintained by Olympic National Park, is such a short trail that it is not often described in hiking guides. It one of those "upside down" trails that descends steeply downhill, and you gain elevation on your way out. The Cox Valley Trail (Hike 3) shares this trait. Because the Cox Valley Trail is a short hike (and a long drive from the Puget Sound area), you can combine it with the P. J. Lake Trail. Hikers enjoy the lake and nearby waterfall in solitude.

From Port Angeles drive the Hurricane Ridge Road, which climbs through foothills to Heart of the Hills entrance station and a campground. In about 17 miles, just before the Hurricane Ridge Visitor Center, make an extremely sharp left-hand turn onto the Obstruction Point Road, which heads downhill. (If you end up at the Hurricane Ridge Visitor Center, you missed the Obstruction Point Road.) Drive 3.7 miles to "Waterhole" and the signed trailhead in a large parking area on the left-hand side of the road, considered the halfway point along the Obstruction Point Road.

The trail begins in a stand of subalpine fir mixed with snags and immediately begins a descent. At less than 0.3 mile there are views across the valley. The trail continues to the edge of an open area with views down the Morse Creek valley to Puget Sound. The trail soon returns to the trees and switchbacks to an open slope (these are avalanche slopes in the winter and spring), where you are within earshot of small streams. Cross the small streams that are bordered by wildflowers in the summer. Early in the hiking season, tiger lilies and paintbrush dominate the landscape. Here, the trail stays level for a way before it approaches the base of a mossy cliff at about 0.8 mile.

The mossy cliff may be the highlight of the hike if you're carrying a camera: a 30-foot waterfall descends the outlet stream from P. J. Lake. A short climb beside the waterfall leads to the north shore of the lake and a campsite. The lake is small and pretty with silver snags; Owl Rock broods above the far end of the lake.

Hikers with scrambling and routefinding skills can explore further, but should have map and compass skills if exploring cross-country. Faint paths can be traced around the lake and beyond, but these are probably game trails.

5 THE BROTHERS CAMP

Distance: 12.4 miles round trip
Difficulty: Moderate
Type of trail: Maintained USFS way trail
Starting point: 700 feet
High point: 3,000 feet
Elevation gain: 2,300 feet
Hikable: Spring, summer, fall
Map: Green Trails No. 168 The Brothers
Information: Hood Canal Ranger District, 360-877-5254
Cautions: Loose rock on summit route, routefinding, avalanche danger early in season

The Brothers were discovered in 1792 by English naval explorer George Vancouver, who saw the peaks from Hood Canal. It was named in 1856 by Captain George Davidson of the U.S. Coast Guard Survey. Davidson was in love with Ellinor Fauntleroy and named the peaks for her brothers, Edward and Arthur, in an attempt to impress her and her father. The Brothers straddle the boundary between Olympic National Park and The Brothers Wilderness in Olympic National Forest.

Hikers enjoy the scenery and views as far as The Brothers Camp but shouldn't venture beyond that point. The route to the south summit is a scramble recommended only for strong, experienced hikers with scrambling and/or climbing skills; the north summit is considered a technical climb. Only the south peak is recommended. The skills required to reach the south summit of The Brothers fall into that gray area between scrambling and climbing. However you define it, the south summit is challenging. Early in the year, avalanche danger is high; when the snow is gone, rockfall is a constant hazard. Helmets are

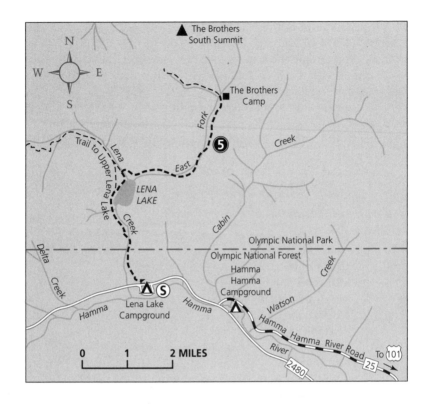

advised and it is best to keep the party small. Routefinding can be a challenge when it is cloudy or foggy. The elevation gain is significant and most parties allow 2 or 3 days. Check with the Hood Canal Ranger District for current conditions beyond The Brothers Camp.

The approach is on the Lower Lena Lake Trailhead in Olympic National Forest. Lena Creek was discovered in 1898 by topographers Arthur Dodwell and Theodore Rixon. This enjoyable route travels through a variety of terrain. The Lower Lena Lake Trail is very popular and you will seldom have it to yourself. The trail was rerouted years ago—traces of the original, steeper trail can still be seen.

From US 101 2.3 miles north of Eldon, take the Hamma Hamma River Road (Forest Road No. 25) west. After you pass the Hamma Hamma Campground at 6 miles, continue to the Lena Lake Trailhead at 7.5 miles.

The trail begins in second-growth forest and enters old growth before approaching Lena Creek. At 1.8 miles cross Lena Creek on a bridge, but don't be surprised if the creek is dry—the water sometimes flows underground. The trail contours beneath cliffs that loom above and provide a sheltered spot in the rain. At 3 miles (2,100 feet), reach the junction with the Upper Lena Lake Trail to the left; stay to the right. The trail drops to 55-acre Lena Lake, with the outlet at the south end. Camps have been closed along the shore here due to overuse (camp on the north side of the lake). The trail passes near a rock formation called Chapel Rock, a favorite lunch stop for hikers because the rock overlooks the lake and is often in the sun. The Lena Lake Trail ends near a junction at the southwest corner of the lake (1,900 feet), 3.4 miles from the trailhead. Turn right for The Brothers Trail.

The Brothers Trail is sometimes defined as a way trail; however, we have always found it to be in good condition despite limited maintenance. The trail has evolved over the years, beaten into shape by climbers. The path crosses Lena Creek on a log bridge, then continues to follow the lakeshore, passing campsites before it enters The Brothers Wilderness and begins to gain elevation.

The trail passes through the poetically named Valley of Silent Men. There are several stories as to how this valley was named, some more intriguing than others. One is that the name evolved during climbing classes held in the 1940s. Climbing students camped at Lena Lake had to get an extremely early start to reach their summit. Because it was usually dark, the students kept their thoughts to themselves and were silent—hence the name. This is one of the prettier sections of the trail as it weaves through great mossy boulders and climbs beside East Fork Lena Creek. As the trail climbs, the valley narrows and there are several crossings of East Fork Lena Creek, each more scenic than the one before, with cascades and dark gorges where the creek has formed pools.

Climbers approaching the south summit

The terrain changes as the trail climbs through a forest of hemlock and silver fir. In August and September this section of trail is favored among yellowjackets. We have never managed to get up or down this section of trail without someone in our party getting stung. At 2.8 miles from the trail junction at the lake (about 6.2 miles from the trailhead), reach The Brothers Camp. The large camping area can accommodate several tents. Water is plentiful.

Beyond the camp, the trail becomes more of a challenge, climbing ever more steeply, and there is a blowdown. Hikers can try to follow the old trail or a flagged bypass. Anticipate routefinding problems. If you cannot find or follow the route, it is best to retreat. When snow is gone, the route is a scramble of steep heather and loose rock; there is some exposure and helmets should be worn. The summit ridge is reached by a final rock scramble. On a clear day the views are impressive: Baker, Shuksan, Glacier Peak, Mount Rainier, Mount St. Helens, even Mount Adams, as well as the Puget Sound basin—downtown Seattle can also be seen. To the west are more Olympic peaks.

6 PUTVIN TRAIL

Distance: 7.2 miles round trip
Difficulty: Challenging
Type of trail: Way trail
Starting point: 1,580 feet
High point: 4,900 feet
Elevation gain: 3,320 feet
Hikable: Summer, fall
Maps: Custom Correct Mount Skokomish–Lake Cushman;
   USGS Mount Skokomish
Information: Hood Canal Ranger District, 360-877-5254;
   Olympic National Park Wilderness Information Center,
   360-565-3100
Cautions: Routefinding, landslides, brush

This is not an easy hike; it is recommended for hikers and backpackers with routefinding skills. Lake of the Angels is nestled in the Valley of Heaven, perhaps so named because you almost have to die to get to it. The trail is relentless and steep. Landslides have added more challenges to the difficult terrain. Strong hikers can hike there in a day, but because Lake of the Angels is one of the premier destinations in

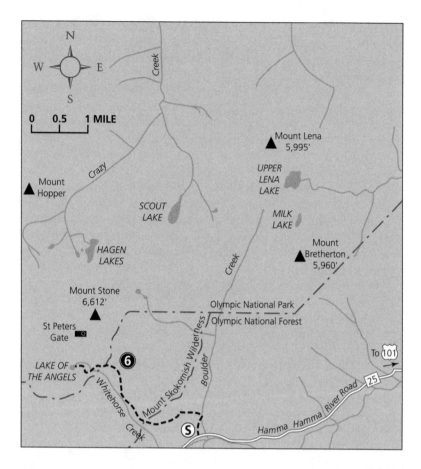

Olympic National Park, a backpacking trip is recommended. You don't need an overnight permit to camp along the Putvin Trail in Olympic National Forest and Mount Skokomish Wilderness, but you do need a wilderness overnight permit if you are going to Lake of the Angels in Olympic National Park. Lake of the Angels is at its best in summer shortly after the snow melts out and the lake is bordered with white avalanche lilies. You'll want to spend time here soaking in the scenery and views, and you will have earned it. Mountain goats frequent the area and are tame enough to lick the salt off your hands if you permit them to. Because mountain goats like salt, be sure to stow your pack inside your tent or they will chew on the pack straps. The goats are attracted to the salt in urine, so hikers should pee on rocks rather than vegetation because otherwise the goats will wallow in the vegetation. Whatever your beliefs are regarding the presence of mountain goats in the Olympics, you can't help but admire their beauty and skill as they navigate rocky faces many climbers wouldn't attempt without a rope.

A base camp near Lake of the Angels sets you up for more options, including a scramble of Mount Skokomish or Mount Stone, a steep climb up to a fearful notch called St. Peters Gate, or an ascent to a pass overlooking Hagen Lakes and the beginning of the Mount Hopper Way Trail (Hike 7). Mount Stone (6,612 feet) was originally named for a member of the 1890 O'Neil expedition, William Marsh, who first sighted the peak; it was named Marsh Peak in his honor. It was later discovered that Marsh was an army deserter by the name of Wiser, but this was not discovered until the completion of the expedition and the peak had already been officially named. After a court-martial of Wiser and his dishonorable discharge, the name of the mountain was changed to Mount Stone because it is stony and rocky.

From US 101 2.3 miles north of Eldon, take the Hamma Hamma River Road (Forest Road No. 25) west. Pass the Hamma Hamma Campground at 6 miles and the Lena Lake Trailhead at 7.5 miles. The road is paved with two lanes to the Lena Lake Trailhead. Continue 3.5 or 4 miles to the Putvin Trailhead. (There is a washout 2 miles past the Putvin Trailhead. According to Olympic National Forest, the slide has been graded but only high-clearance vehicles should attempt to cross the washout. Drive at your own risk.)

The trail begins by climbing over rocky terrain between Boulder Creek and an old logging road, crossing the road and continuing into the Mount Skokomish Wilderness at 1.3 miles. From here, as you climb you hear Whitehorse Creek, though the stream is obscured. The trail nears the creek, turns right, and continues to switchback steeply through forest before leveling out into more open terrain. At about 2.2 miles a side trail on the left descends to a campsite near the creek; stay right.

The trail stays level for a way as it crosses a basin with a healthy population of slide alder, vine maple, and ferns. As the trail begins to climb the headwall, it becomes more of a challenge and can be hazardous. The trail is exposed and eroded, and you may be hanging on to roots, fallen trees, and bushes. This section of trail could almost be described as a scramble, because scrambling skills may be needed to get past this stretch. Once you are over the headwall, the going is easier as the trail follows along the rim of the headwall and drops to a small stream at about 3 miles. In late summer this is a good spot to graze on huckleberries; you are within sight and sound of Whitehorse Creek.

Pond behind Mount Stone

The trail comes to a pond, and first-timers heave a sigh of relief thinking they've reached the lake, but don't set your pack down yet. The pond is aptly named Pond of the False Prophet. This very scenic spot, with Mount Stone to the north and Mount Skokomish to the southwest, is where the trail enters Olympic National Park and meadowlands.

The trail crosses the creek and climbs through masses of wildflowers, continuing along Whitehorse Creek and leveling out. As you cross Whitehorse Creek at about 3.3 miles, Lake of the Angels is ahead at 3.6 miles, nestled in the Valley of Heaven. The lake is situated in a glacial cirque below the ridge that links Mount Stone and Mount Skokomish. Mount Skokomish rises from the shores of the lake, and on the north side of the lake, steep slopes lead to Mount Stone.

The trail officially ends at the lake, but experienced scramblers will find many other delights. A way trail climbs to the ridge between Mount Stone and Mount Skokomish with views to the west of Ducka-bush and Steel, Chimney Peak and Mount Hopper, Puget Sound and Hood Canal. Beyond is the beginning of the Mount Hopper Way Trail (Hike 7). On the skyline is St. Peters Gate (5,900 feet), a notch in the southwest ridge of Mount Stone.

7 MOUNT HOPPER WAY TRAIL

Distance: 36.2 miles round trip to Great Stone Arrow
Difficulty: Challenging
Type of trail: Maintained NPS way trail
Starting point: 800 feet
High point: 5,350 feet
Elevation gain: 4,550 feet
Hikable: Summer, fall
Maps: Custom Correct Mount Skokomish–Lake Cushman;
USGS Mount Skokomish
Information: Olympic National Park Wilderness
Information Center, 360-565-3100
Cautions: Routefinding, scrambling

This is not a day hike by any stretch of the imagination. Most of the trails in this book can be done in a day, but this is such exceptionally beautiful country that, even though it is a backpacking trip, it is worth including. The first 12 miles, on the North Fork Skokomish Trail in Olympic National Park, are maintained and not difficult. Much of the route, which stays level, coincides with the route taken by the 1890 O'Neil expedition. The hard work doesn't begin until you approach the First Divide and turn off onto the Mount Hopper Way Trail. Here the challenges truly begin, because the trail gets very little (if any) maintenance. Harsh winters and heavy snowfalls have taken their toll. Game trails add to the confusion and finding the route is not easy. The way trail beyond First Divide is recommended for only extremely strong and experienced backpackers with scrambling and routefinding skills. A backcountry permit is needed for any overnight camping in Olympic National Park. Call the Olympic National Park Wilderness Information Center for details on fees, permits, reservations, and regulations.

Drive US 101 to Hoodsport along Hood Canal. At Hoodsport turn uphill onto Lake Cushman Road and continue 9 miles to a junction. Turn left on Forest Service Road No. 24 and follow the lakeshore to Staircase Ranger Station and the North Fork Skokomish Trailhead.

The first few miles of trail are on an old road (closed in 1973 because it was difficult to maintain) that begins as a gentle climb with overlooks above the Skokomish River and continues through old-growth forest of Douglas fir, red cedar, and hemlock. The trail goes through a section that was hit by a forest fire—the Beaver Fire—in 1985

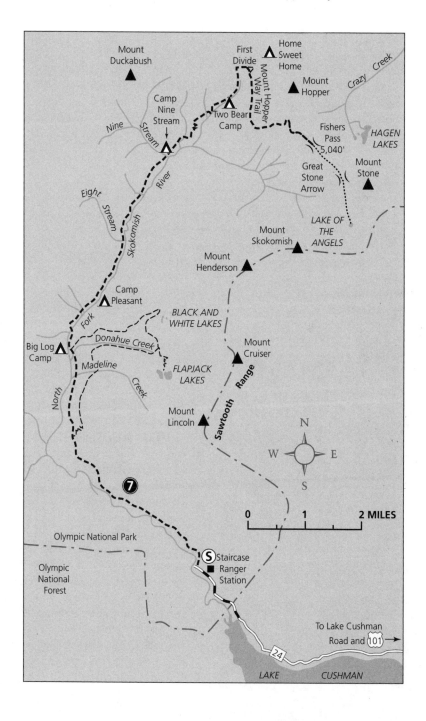

that destroyed 1,400 acres of timber. At 3.8 miles reach the junction for the Flapjack Lakes Trail on the right; stay left. The North Fork Skokomish Trail crosses Madeline Creek, then Donahue Creek. At 5.6 miles is the junction for the Black and White Lakes Way Trail on the right; stay left. Shortly after, a path to the left descends to Big Log Camp, a popular campsite; stay right. The trail continues to Camp Pleasant, at 7.1 miles (1,600 feet), a very pretty but very popular campsite. The trail then crosses Eight Stream and, at 10 miles, Nine Stream, where Camp Nine Stream is located (2,000 feet); the O'Neil expedition had one of its camps here.

From here the trail, mostly level to this point, switchbacks steeply through forest. At 12 miles the trail comes to Two Bear Camp, named in 1924 by the foreman of the trail crew because the men often spotted two bears in the meadows above. The trail turns right and contours beneath the ridge to the junction with the Mount Hopper Way Trail on the right at 13.1 miles (4,540 feet). Going left up to First Divide is worth a side trip—it involves a short ascent of 148 feet in less than 0.25 mile to First Divide, an excellent lunch spot (4,688 feet) with views down to Home Sweet Home nestled in rich meadows.

The burn on Mount Hopper

It is just about impossible to give a detailed route description of the Mount Hopper Way Trail because conditions change from year to year and maintenance is limited. The trail has many ups and downs as it traverses around the western and southern sides of Mount Hopper. Windfalls and game trails add confusion, and the trail tends to fade out in meadows. As the trail alternates between forest and meadows, the meadows predominate as you near the end of the route. From the open areas there are views of Mount Skokomish and Mount Henderson. The trail climbs and ends at Fishers Pass (5,040 feet) in 2 miles from the junction near First Divide (15.1 miles from the trailhead). The pass overlooks Elk Basin (named by the O'Neil expedition because they found a herd of elk here and killed several) at the head of Crazy Creek. Purportedly one can hike from here north to the summit of Mount Hopper by following the south ridge, but we were unable to find the route.

Beyond the pass, the trail is even more indistinct and hard to follow as it goes southeast through a section that was devastated by forest fire. The route essentially follows the ridge between Mount Hopper and Mount Stone to the Great Stone Arrow (5,350 feet) at 5 miles from the junction near First Divide (18.1 miles from the trailhead). The Great Stone Arrow—a high pass at the base of Mount Stone between the headwaters of the North Fork Skokomish and a branch of Crazy Creek that begins in Hagen Lakes (the lakes lie on the north side of Mount Stone)—is a worthy goal; it is so named because rocks have been placed to form a directional arrow.

Beyond the Great Stone Arrow, experienced scramblers can descend a primitive route to Lake of the Angels and exit at the Putvin Trail (Hike 6) for an unusual and challenging loop hike that will provide enough memories to last a lifetime.

8 DRY CREEK TRAIL

Distance: 7.2 miles round trip to bridge; 14 miles round trip to upper trailhead
Difficulty: Moderate
Type of trail: Maintained/occasionally maintained USFS trail
Starting elevation: 750 feet
High point: 1,543 feet at bridge; 3,650 feet at high pass
Elevation gain: 800 feet to bridge; 2,900 feet to high pass
Hikable: Spring, summer, fall
Maps: Green Trails No. 199 Mount Tebo; Custom Correct Mount Skokomish–Lake Cushman
Information: Olympic National Forest (Hood Canal), 360-877-5254
Cautions: Stream crossings, routefinding, blowdowns

The Dry Creek Trail is overlooked by most hikers. Though it can often be hiked year-round, it doesn't get a lot of attention. It is part of a trail system that once began from the Staircase Ranger Station in Olympic National Park and continued to Camp Comfort on the South Fork

Skokomish River. The trail now begins at the upper end of Lake Cushman on the other side of the causeway. The stumps in the lake are from big trees that were cut when the town of Tacoma built a dam on the North Fork Skokomish in the 1920s. Building the dam resulted in enlarging the lake. When Lake Cushman is low, the upper end of the lake is dry. There is nothing pristine about stumps around the lakeshore, but stick with this trail—it gets better. Despite the eerie quality the stumps give to the lake, Mount Rose (4,301 feet) rises triumphantly above it. Look close, though, and you can see where a forest fire once marched up the slopes of the mountain.

Most hikers won't get to the end of the 7-mile trail through Olympic National Forest, stopping instead at about the halfway point where Dry Creek must be crossed. Here a crucial bridge was badly damaged and needs to be replaced. If the stream is running high, hikers shouldn't attempt to use the hazardous bridge. But up to the damaged bridge, this is an easy hike with solitude and views; it is especially pleasant in spring or early summer. The trail climbs through second-growth forest with cedar stumps left from logging days, alders, and early spring flowers—trilliums, yellow violets, Indian plum, and salmonberry. The beginning of the trail hints of rain-forest ambience before climbing into second growth.

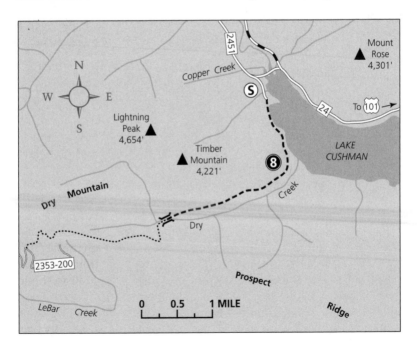

The broken bridge over Dry Creek

Drive US 101 to Hoodsport along Hood Canal. At Hoodsport turn uphill onto Lake Cushman Road and continue 9 miles to a junction. Turn left on Forest Road No. 24 and drive about 2.7 miles, following along the lake to Forest Road No. 2451 (Lightning Peak Road); turn left onto FR 2451, which crosses a causeway to the west side of the Skokomish River. The trailhead is on the other side of the causeway.

The trail begins as a cat track near Lake Cushman and summer homes. There are views of the lake through the trees, but initial views may be somewhat disappointing. At about 0.4 mile the road becomes more trail-like, and signs for Dry Creek guide you through the labyrinth of driveways and private lanes. The trail climbs away from the lake to meet an old logging road. At about 1.4 miles, a side trail to the left descends to a campsite near the lake; stay right. The trail continues to climb at a moderate grade through second-growth forest. As the trail levels off, the dark forest is brightened by stands of alder, and Dry Creek can be heard below. At 3.6 miles the trail reaches the damaged bridge; this is a good turnaround for most hikers, though Dry Creek is not difficult to ford in late summer when the water level is low.

The trail continues on the other side of the creek, but maintenance is limited. At about 4 miles the trail enters old-growth forest of western red cedar, silver fir, and hemlock, climbing to Prospect Ridge (3,000 feet), where logging activity is evident. The trail continues along the ridge and at about 6 miles reaches a high pass (3,650 feet) between Dry Mountain and the western end of Prospect Ridge. The trail descends into a basin at the head of LeBar Creek and ends at Forest Road No. 2353-200 (3,200 feet) about 7 miles from the trailhead near Lake Cushman.

Old-growth tree and wildflowers in the North Cascades

STATE ROUTE 20/
RAINY PASS

9 NEWHALEM CREEK TRAIL

Distance: 9 miles round trip to Newhalem Camp
Difficulty: Moderate
Type of trail: Occasionally maintained NPS trail
Starting point: 1,000 feet
High point: 1,800 feet
Elevation gain: 800 feet
Hikable: Year-round
Maps: Green Trails No. 16 Ross Lake, No. 48 Diablo Dam
Information: North Cascades National Park, 360-856-5700
Cautions: Brush

This quiet trail, an old logging road that is becoming more trail-like with each passing year, follows a forested valley near Newhalem Creek in Ross Lake National Recreation Area and North Cascades National Park. This old trail is not featured in many hiking guides, nor was there a sign at the trailhead in the spring of 2000. Park Service personnel and volunteers occasionally brush out the first mile of the trail, but for the most part the trail is left to nature's whims; alders and brush are taking over the trail. Spring and fall rather than summer are the best times to hike the trail due to the brush; the trail is at its best in October when the leaves of the deciduous trees turn golden. There are views of Newhalem Creek along the beginning of the trail. For most hikers the metal bridge at 1.8 miles will be far enough. There is a major washout at 3.8 miles that may necessitate turning around, depending on conditions and strength of the party. Volunteers work on this trail from time to time—call North Cascades National Park to find out trail conditions and whether the washout has been repaired or bypassed. From Newhalem Camp, experienced climbers and scramblers with routefinding skills can access Stout Lake and other high-country gems on cross-country routes.

From Interstate 5 at Burlington, take State Route 20 east to just before you reach the town of Newhalem. Just beyond the bridge over Goodell Creek, at the road to the North Cascades Visitor Center (it is well signed), turn right. Cross the Skagit River on a bridge, pass outbuildings, and turn left (uphill) on an unsigned gravel road. Drive 2.2 miles to the end of the road and the trailhead. There are no facilities. You can request directions, if needed, at the visitor center, open daily spring through fall and on weekends in winter.

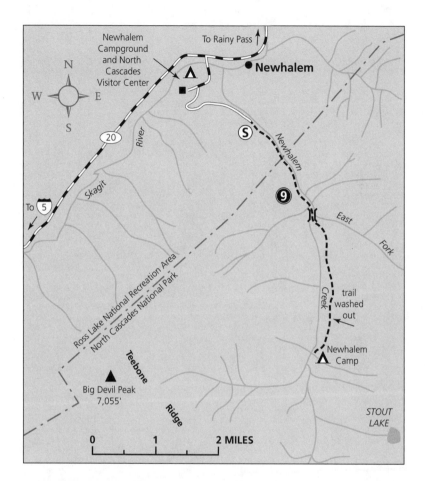

The trail starts within Ross Lake National Recreation Area and at 0.75 mile enters North Cascades National Park, closely following Newhalem Creek for about 2 miles. The trail stays level; this section is a pleasant winter walk when the brush has died back. Through the trees there are also emerging views of high ridges and the occasional peak. Then, just when you think you've left civilization far behind, you encounter a sturdy metal bridge at 1.8 miles. At first glance this bridge in the middle of nowhere is shocking, but this was once a logging road and such bridges were built to endure. The bridge makes a good turnaround spot for casual hikers, but there is more.

After crossing the creek on the metal bridge, the trail climbs on the east side of the creek. If the clouds are not low in the valley, there

A party of hikers from The Mountaineers on the Newhalem Creek Trail

are views of Little Devil Peak and Big Devil Peak. Teebone Ridge can also be seen from here. The views continue to improve at 2.3 miles, but there is much to see along the way. In fall look for club moss and a variety of colorful mushrooms. In another 1.5 miles you come to a section where the road has washed out and, depending on conditions, you may want to stop here at 3.8 miles.

Hikers have to clamber down into and up the other side of the washout if they want to continue. Beyond the washout the road-trail comes to a junction of roads. To complete the hike, turn right as the trail descends into forest at the old campsite of Newhalem Camp at 4.5 miles.

10 STETATTLE CREEK

Distance: 4 miles round trip to Camp Dayo Creek
Difficulty: Moderate
Type of trail: Occasionally maintained NPS trail
Starting point: 900 feet
High point: 1,500 feet
Elevation gain: 600 feet
Hikable: Spring, summer, fall
Map: Green Trails No. 48 Diablo Dam
Information: North Cascades National Park, 360-856-5700
Cautions: Avalanches early in season, stream crossings, brush beyond 2.5 miles

Hikers will find this a good trail for solitude in Ross Lake National Recreation Area and North Cascades National Park because most hikers pass this up on their way to nearby Sourdough Mountain or loftier pursuits. Hikers willing to battle brush may find traces of an old trail that once led into the Picket Range. This trail deep in the mountains was a common route used by mountaineers on their way to climb McMillan Spires and Davis Peak. Davis Peak, first climbed in 1904 by surveyors for the U.S. Geological Survey, is seldom climbed today because of the rugged approach. Rumors persist of a way trail that climbs to Azure Lake. Before Diablo Dam was constructed by Seattle City Light, the canyon was a deep, narrow gorge through which torrents of water poured from the snowfields of the North Cascades.

Stetattle Creek is a good destination in the North Cascades when the high country is snowed in, because the starting elevation is only 900 feet. The trail can often be hiked in winter if the snow level is not too low. October may be the most enjoyable time to hike the trail—the fall colors are brilliant, the streams are easy to cross, and there are a

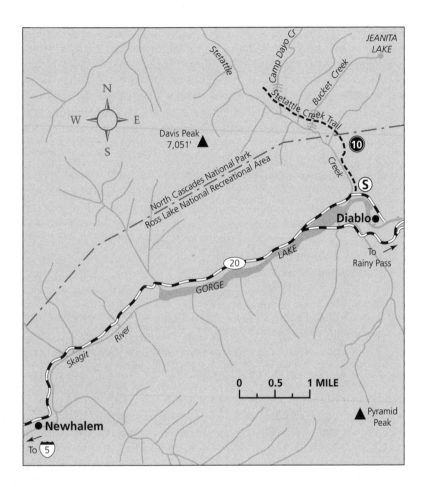

variety of mushrooms. Vine maple is vibrant along Stetattle Creek, and hikers enjoy a variety of evergreens as the trail climbs deeper into the valley. The diverse forest community includes western red cedar, mountain hemlock, red alder, and big leaf maple. The damp climate provides an ideal environment for club moss. The trail never really leaves the forest, so you have to fight brush for views that are few and far between, but the trail has a quiet beauty of its own. In summer there are many ideal picnic spots along Stetattle Creek, especially within the first 0.5 mile. Choose from a variety of rocks to sit upon to view the creek and watch for water ouzels (American dippers), small waterbirds that forage in creeks. Stetattle Creek is closed to fishing from its mouth to Bucket Creek. In summer and fall the length of the trail

(2.25 miles) is easy to hike. In spring or late fall, stream crossings can present a challenge, especially during periods of rain or melt-off. There are several stream crossings—each one is different. Depending on conditions and time of year, some of the streams can be crossed on logs; others are mere hops, skips, and jumps.

From Interstate 5, drive State Route 20 through Marblemount and Newhalem; just before the Gorge Lake bridge near milepost 126, turn left and drive toward the small town of Diablo. Find the trailhead just beyond the Stetattle Creek bridge. Park in the small turnout to the right.

The trail parallels Stetattle Creek for the first 0.6 mile. The big chunk of concrete lying in the creek is the site of river gauging stations and a cable car. At this point the trail climbs a hillside. The trail leaves Ross Lake National Recreation Area at 1 mile and enters North Cascades National Park. The trail crosses more small creeks as it passes through an open forest of lodgepole pine and salal, the result of a forest fire in the 1900s. Here are views of Davis Peak through the trees. Bucket Creek Falls is reached at about 1.4 miles. On a clear day you

Stetattle Creek

can look down the valley for views of Pyramid and Colonial Peaks.

The trail crosses several more creeks, but becomes more difficult to follow as the tread grows fainter. Between Bucket Creek Falls and Camp Dayo Creek, the trail shows fewer signs of maintenance. There is a major blowdown across the trail, and huckleberry bushes obscure the route. The somewhat-maintained trail continues to Camp Dayo Creek at about 2 miles, where the trail crosses beneath a waterfall. Diehards can follow faint tread another 0.25 mile beyond the waterfall, but the trail ends inexplicably in a tangle of brush and flagging near a fallen cedar serving as a nurse log. Only explorers with a high tolerance for putting up with brush will want to venture beyond this point.

11 RUBY MOUNTAIN

Distance: 19 miles round trip
Difficulty: Challenging
Type of trail: Maintained/abandoned NPS trail
Starting point: 1,200 feet
High point: 7,408 feet
Elevation gain: Approximately 6,200 feet
Hikable: Summer, fall
Maps: Green Trails No. 48 Diablo Dam, No. 49 Mount Logan
Information: North Cascades National Park Wilderness Information Center, 360-873-4590 ext. 39
Cautions: Blowdowns, routefinding, avalanche danger early in season

Ruby Mountain, in Ross Lake National Recreation Area east of the south arm of Diablo Lake and 2.8 miles southeast of Ross Dam, rises above Thunder Arm, with small glaciers on its northeast side. It was first climbed in 1934. In 1970 when the National Park Service and the U.S. Forest Service released preliminary plans for development of North Cascades National Park/National Recreation Area complex, an aerial tramway was proposed from the North Cascades Highway to the summit of Ruby Mountain, but these plans were abandoned. There were also provisions for an aerial tram from Arctic Creek on Ross Lake that would have extended into the Pickets, and a hostel was planned at Bridge Creek. None of these plans were ever developed.

The Ruby Mountain Trail is no longer described in current hiking

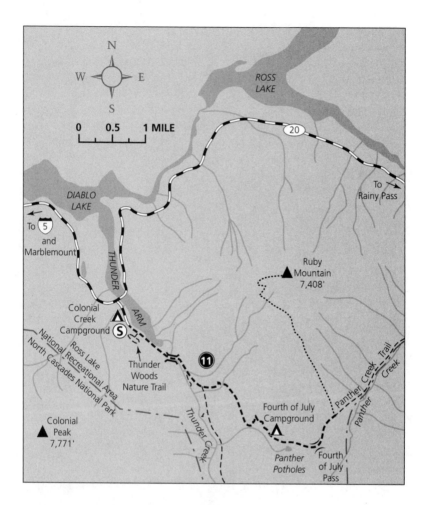

guides, but it can be found in older guidebooks. The trail was abandoned in 1973, though scramblers and hikers continue to use it. Hikers sometimes find the trail by accident, as we did. We had hiked up to Fourth of July Pass from Thunder Creek and continued past a small, stagnant pond about 0.5 mile from the pass, where we noticed a faint trail going off to the left. We followed the trail until we came to a sign that informed us the trail was no longer maintained (the sign cannot be seen from the trail). We hiked about 1 mile until we lost the trail in a blowdown. This was the old trail to Ruby Mountain. Later, on a Mountaineers scramble of Ruby Mountain, the leader followed a compass bearing rather than the old trail. We found several sections of the trail as we climbed, and

followed the trail down on our descent. Most hikers prefer the abandoned trail to the scramble route. Others had also rediscovered (or already knew) of the trail, and soon a route was flagged through the blowdown. However, it is no longer considered politically correct to flag a route, and rangers removed the flagging in 2000.

Today the trail is easier to follow because it gets more use, though conditions change from year to year. Strong hikers with routefinding skills enjoy the views and solitude. Most hikers will want to do this as a backpacking trip because it is 2,100 feet of elevation gain just to get to Fourth of July Pass (though strong hikers have done it in a day). Obtain the required free backcountry permit at the Wilderness Information Center in Marblemount, at the end of Ranger Station Road, 1 mile off the North Cascades Highway/State Route 20. Water is not available beyond the pass, so carry water if you are continuing to Ruby Mountain.

From Interstate 5, drive east on SR 20 past Marblemount and Newhalem to Colonial Creek Campground near milepost 130. Begin on the Thunder Creek Trail from near the amphitheater in the campground.

The trail follows the Thunder Arm of Diablo Lake and crosses Thunder Creek on a bridge at 1 mile. Hike another mile or so to the Fourth of July Pass junction at 2.1 miles and turn left (uphill). The trail climbs 2.5 miles in steady switchbacks to Fourth of July Campground (3,400 feet) at 4.6 miles, where there are partial views of Colonial and Snowfield Peaks to the west. A bit farther is a knoll with views of Colonial, Snowfield, Tricouni, Primus, and to the south a piece of Buckner and the Boston Glacier.

For Ruby Mountain, continue east. The trail loses some elevation and passes above the Panther Potholes on your right, reaching Fourth of July Pass (3,600 feet) at 5.3 miles. The main trail now becomes the Panther Creek Trail, which descends to State Route 20 in about 5 miles. The unmarked trail to Ruby Mountain is found about 0.6 mile east of Fourth of July Pass at 5.9 miles, just beyond the stagnant tarn that may be dry later in the season. The trail crosses a stream east of the pond (neither stream nor pond are shown on maps). Just past the creek, find the "UNMAINTAINED TRAIL" sign. From here it is approximately 3.6 miles to the summit of Ruby.

The blowdown is reached in about a mile, 6.9 miles from the trailhead, but beyond the blowdown the trail is in fairly good condition. Where tread is faint, look for blazes or flagging. Good views begin at about 5,000 feet. The trail eventually leaves the forest on the

A hiker on Ruby Mountain waits for the clouds to lift.

west side of Ruby at about 7.4 miles, and stays level for about 0.5 mile. At 7.9 miles the trail switchbacks up a steep meadow where hikers are rewarded with magnificent views of Colonial Peak, Pyramid Peak, Mount Baker, and Mount Shuksan. The trail is vague and hard to follow in the meadow, but you can see the ridge crest.

Proceed northwest up the meadow about 1 mile to the obvious saddle between two high points at about 7,300 feet. Turn left (north) and follow the ridge about 0.25 mile to the summit at 9.5 miles. The last 50 feet are on talus. From the summit the views are impressive— Ross Lake, Jack Mountain, the Pickets, Colonial, and Hozomeen Peak. In addition to the views from the summit, hikers also encounter a radio repeater—a large solar-paneled communication device used by Park Service personnel. Do not tamper with the radio repeater because park communications are highly dependent on this structure.

The trail up Ruby Mountain can also be reached from the Panther Creek Trailhead, which begins 8 miles to the east of Colonial Creek Campground off SR 20. A Northwest Forest Pass is required at this trailhead (parking is actually at the trailhead for the East Bank Trail on the other side of the highway, just west across from the Panther Creek bridge). The 5-mile Panther Creek Trail is often washed out early in the season, so check with North Cascades National Park before you start.

12   EAST CREEK TRAIL

Distance: 16 miles round trip to Mebee Pass
Difficulty: Challenging
Type of trail: Maintained/occasionally maintained USFS trail
Starting point: 2,350 feet
High point: 6,700 feet
Elevation gain: Approximately 4,350 feet
Hikable: Summer, fall
Maps: Green Trails No. 49 Mount Logan; USGS Azurite
  Peak
Information: Methow Valley Visitor Center, 509-997-2131
  (closed in winter)
Cautions: Brush beyond 4.5 miles, obscure route, stream
  crossings

The seldom-hiked East Creek Trail in Okanogan–Wenatchee National Forest is closed to motor bikes. This long trail is probably best done as a backpacking trip because it climbs to Mebee Pass at 8.3 miles and then descends to meet the headwaters of the West Fork Methow River. Hikers enjoy old mines, scenery, and solitude—there were no other cars at this trailhead when we came in mid-August, the peak of the hiking season in the North Cascades.

From Interstate 5, drive east on State Route 20 to 15 miles east of Colonial Creek Campground (at milepost 130). The trailhead for East Creek Trail No. 756 is signed.

The trail begins by crossing Granite Creek on a sturdy bridge, then climbs through lodgepole pine to a viewpoint of Beebe Mountain (to the west) at about 1 mile. Beebe Mountain was named for Frank Beebe,

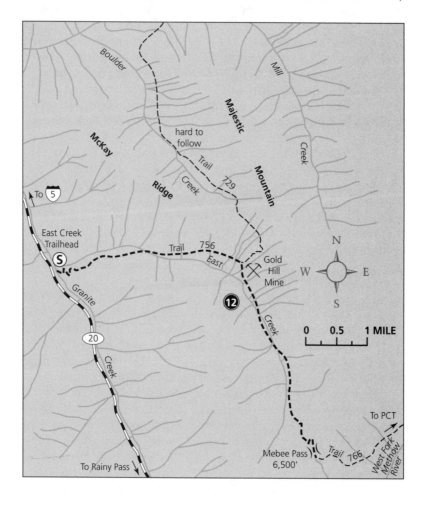

an early prospector. A small boulder field is crossed before the trail rounds the ridge onto slopes above East Creek. Lodgepole pine is replaced by mossy forest of mainly hemlock. The trail continues a gradual climb through forest to an unbridged crossing of East Creek at 2.2 miles and campsites. In 2000 a log was in place for the crossing, which can be hazardous when the stream is running high. Beyond, the trail continues to climb through cool forest, following the creek eastward and crossing several small streams before reaching an unsigned trail junction at 4 miles. Unsigned and abandoned Boulder Creek Trail No. 729 climbs uphill to the left; stay straight.

(Trail reconstruction for the Boulder Creek Trail is in the works. In 2000 a short climb led to private property, where we turned around, though it appeared the trail could be picked up on the other side. The trail is shown as a primitive trail on the USGS Azurite Peak map, 1963, and is also shown on the Green Trails map. Coming from Canyon Creek, the Boulder Creek Trail follows an old narrow-gauge road to the North American Mine site, then climbs up the valley over a pass to meet the East Creek Trail. According to a recent report, the trail is brushy and difficult to follow at the head of Boulder Creek. This trail was last cleared in 1980 according to old hiking guides.)

For Mebee Pass continue straight as the trail levels out at the site of the Gold Hill Mine. This is a good spot for day hikers to turn around. There are views and artifacts to photograph. Look for the timbers of collapsed structures and the rusting equipment of mining days. Though the first 4 miles of trail are maintained and in good condition, beyond the Gold Hill Mine the trail is brushy and hard to follow. The trail gets limited maintenance beyond this point, and finding the route can be a challenge because the trail crosses several brushy avalanche slopes. If you lose the trail, head downhill toward the bottom of the valley, even though it might seem more logical to contour. Though it defies logic, the old trail drops straight downhill a short distance beyond the mine site, crosses a small stream, then levels off near the valley bottom. The trail crosses more avalanche slopes and pockets of forest before it enters a meadow and continues its descent to East Creek. This was as far as we hiked.

Here East Creek must be forded and at times fording may be impossible depending on season and conditions. According to old hiking guides and trail reports, the trail ascends into a brushy avalanche chute on the west side of East Creek and crosses back to the east bank. The trail continues through forest to the head of the valley, where the forest is interrupted by more avalanche paths. The final switchbacks to

Abandoned mining equipment near the Gold Hill Mine

the pass are short and steep as the trail enters a small basin beneath the pass. Larch trees replace hemlock and Douglas firs, and the slopes are covered with blueberry and heather. The trail climbs to Mebee Pass at 8.3 miles, with views of Holliway Mountain and Golden Horn. Scramblers can continue north to the ridgeline to look for the remains of a lookout dating from the 1930s.

Mebee Pass can also be approached from the Pacific Crest Trail (PCT). A spur trail, Trail No. 766, leads 8 miles from the PCT to the pass.

Fall foliage along the Mountain Loop Highway

MOUNTAIN LOOP HIGHWAY

13   NEIDERPRUM TRAIL

Distance: 5 miles round trip
Difficulty: Moderate
Type of trail: Occasionally maintained USFS way trail
Starting point: 800 feet
High point: 4,400 feet (meadow below pass)
Elevation gain: 3,600 feet
Hikable: Summer, fall
Maps: Green Trails No. 89 Darrington; USGS Silverton
Information: Darrington Ranger Station, 360-436-1155
Cautions: Steep, rough trail, avalanche danger

Neiderprum Trail No. 653 is an old miners' trail in the Boulder River Wilderness, and it's also known as the Lone Tree Pass trail. It is often used by climbers on their way to Whitehorse Mountain (6,872 feet), which dominates the skyline near Darrington. It is close enough to town that sometimes residents can watch climbing parties from their living room windows. The Native Americans knew the mountain as *So-bahli-ahli*, and when the mountain was fogged in, they knew rain was coming.

Mines were active on the mountain by the 1890s—gold and silver were both discovered. The trail was originally built by Mat Neiderprum. He constructed the trail to reach his limestone claims, and built a cabin and toolshed at 4,400 feet in a meadow near a rocky knoll. Nothing of the cabin remains today. Keith Markwell, who has hiked and climbed in the area for many years, wrote in personal correspondence, "Of all the trails up the north and northwest side of Whitehorse, not a one was intended as a route to the summit; they all just led to mineral prospects, and most converged at Lone Tree Pass." Virgil Peterson, who also climbed extensively in the area, described in a personal letter the route as it was in the 1930s: "It involved driving straight west of Darrington until the road ended in about 2 or 3 miles at Squire Creek. There was a small ranch there; the old bearded rancher might have been Neiderprum. The trail went through a beautiful forest for several miles, then up the mountain in switchbacks. We got as far that day as Lone Tree Pass . . . before reaching Lone Tree Pass there were remains of an old camp, maybe a prospector's camp, which may have been Neiderprum's."

Today the trail to Lone Tree Pass is used more by climbers than hikers; it is appropriate for hikers and scramblers (an ice ax is recommended in early season). The trail is rough and steep, gaining 3,600 feet of elevation in 2.5 miles. The Everett branch of The Mountaineers has maintained the first 1.5 miles or so of the trail. The hike sometimes appears as Lone Tree Pass in hiking guides, and in older hiking guides even appears as Whitehorse Mountain.

From Interstate 5 drive east on State Route 530 through Arlington toward Darrington. About 2 miles past the turnoff for French Creek Campground (about 5 miles west of Darrington), turn right on Mine Road, pass a few houses, and drive to the end of the pavement at 0.5 mile. Turn left on Forest Road 2030 (signed as of October 2000) and drive 2 miles to the road end and trailhead. There are no facilities.

The first mile of trail is wide and easy to follow, though the elevation gain cannot be taken out of the trail. At about 0.5 mile, the trail enters the Boulder River Wilderness (about 1,700 feet). Most of this section has been logged in the past, and giant cedar stumps dominate the steep hillsides in the green gloom of the forest. Shortly beyond the wilderness boundary, old growth takes over and huge cedars are found growing on the steep slopes. At about 1.5 miles, small pockets of forest begin to alternate with open areas.

The trail crosses a small talus field that is a blaze of vine maple in October. An ancient big leaf maple dominates the scene. Although views are subdued on cloudy days, hikers get at least partial views down to the valley. Where a few large trees have fallen across the trail, volunteers have made cuts in the trees for hikers to use as steps. One of the open areas appears to have been hit by a landslide, but a new trail has already been stomped in by eager feet, and volunteers have put in rudimentary rock retaining walls where needed. The route is fairly easy to follow to about 2,800 feet. Beyond that point, the rough, steep trail may seem more like a gully than a trail, but ribbons can be followed. When it gets too rough or the snow too deep, hikers should turn around.

At about 2 miles you'll reach a small stream (about 3,300 feet), where a large log points uphill, with flagging in two directions. The downhill route appears to go to a viewpoint and possible campsite; stay on the uphill route, which continues toward Lone Tree Pass. Experienced scramblers with ice-ax skills can carry on farther, but avalanches are a threat in spring. At about 2.25 miles cross a stream, the last water you'll

Fall colors seen along the Neiderprum Trail

find on the trail. At about 2.5 miles reach the meadow where Neider-prum's cabin once stood. A rocky knoll makes an excellent perch for hikers to enjoy the views down to the valley and to the ice fields of Whitehorse to the south and Mount Higgins and other peaks of the North Cascades to the north. This is where most hikers should stop.

Climbers and those with scrambling skills continue to Lone Tree Pass (when it is snowfree) and beyond the pass on steep snow.

14 HUCKLEBERRY MOUNTAIN TRAIL

Distance: 12 miles round trip to viewpoint
Difficulty: Challenging
Type of trail: Occasionally maintained USFS trail
Starting point: 1,000 feet
High point: 5,483 feet at viewpoint
Elevation gain: 4,483 feet
Hikable: Spring, summer, fall
Maps: Green Trails No. 79 Snow King; USGS Huckleberry Mountain
Information: Darrington Ranger Station, 360-436-1155
Cautions: Snow early in season, blowdowns, routefinding

Huckleberry Mountain Trail No. 780 is one of the steepest trails in the Darrington district of Mount Baker–Snoqualmie National Forest. It was constructed in 1935 to reach a fire lookout and was destroyed by fire in 1962. Ceramic insulators are still occasionally seen on trees from telephone wire that was strung to reach the lookout. History buffs with cross-country hiking/backpacking and routefinding skills can explore a section of abandoned trail that was constructed to connect with the Buck Creek trail in the 1930s. The project was never completed, though the projected trails appear on old maps.

Huckleberry Mountain dropped out of guidebooks for several years, and though it is described in current hiking guides, it doesn't get much use. Because the trail lies outside the Glacier Peak Wilderness and the upper section is becoming overgrown, the trail is included here in the hope that more hikers will use it. Human presence helps keep trails from becoming overgrown and abandoned. The trail covers a variety of terrain. Most of the trail stays in forest that to date has never been logged. The lower sections of trail consist of old-growth Douglas fir and hemlock with zones of hardwoods interspersed at lower elevations.

The higher elevations are parklands that provide generous views of peaks and glaciers.

From Interstate 5, drive State Route 530 east through Arlington and Darrington, then north to where it crosses the Sauk River. Just across the river where SR 530 continues north, go right/straight ahead on Suiattle River Road (Forest Road 26). Drive east 14.5 miles to just beyond Huckleberry Mountain Trail No. 780 and look for a small parking area. There are no facilities.

The trail switchbacks up; in a little more than 1 mile you reach a double waterfall (about 2,050 feet). The first 2.5 miles of the trail have been maintained by Washington Trails Association, and the trail is easy to follow for the first 3.5 miles (to about 3,800 feet), though recent blowdowns have made the trail more challenging. In the first

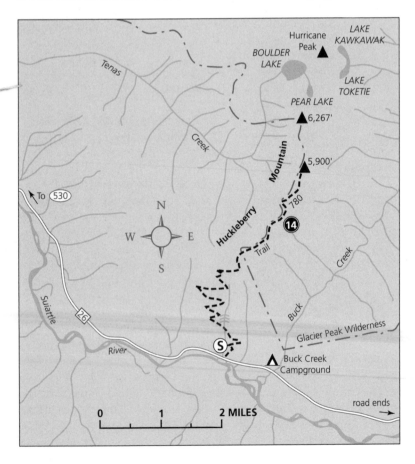

Buck Creek

3.5 miles there are several stream crossings. In about 4 miles the trail passes Fred Bugner Camp, with a water source nearby. The campsite is signed, but the camp is dark and not terribly inviting.

The upper section is often brushy later in the season. At about 4 miles (just before 4,600 feet) the trail comes to a "GLACIER PEAK WILDERNESS" sign, but the trail doesn't enter the wilderness area, it hovers on the edge of it. At about 5 miles the trail levels off to contour beneath a ridge crest and views of White Chuck Mountain. The trail enters meadows and reaches a high point at about 6 miles (5,483 feet). From the high point, look west to the logging roads of Tenas Creek and east to the protected forests of Buck Creek. Green, Buckindy, and Snowking Mountains can also be seen to the east and north. If the lookout site is your objective, you have more work to do: In another mile the trail drops 400 feet before climbing 800 feet to the lookout site at 5,900 feet.

Old maps provide enticing hints of abandoned trails for those who wish to explore further. A 1938 Stillaguamish-Sauk-Suiattle Recreational Areas map (U.S. Forest Service) shows the Huckleberry Mountain Trail making a large loop climbing between Tenas Creek and Big Creek from the Suiattle River Road. Logging roads now intersect this land, but it is possible that some segments of the old trail remain. The 1938 USGS map shows a trail junction below Boulder Lake with a trail leading to the lake and the main trail continuing to Huckleberry Mountain and exiting near Buck Creek Camp and Guard Station (apparently this section of trail was never completed). The 1899 USGS Glacier Peak map designates the area between Big Creek and Tenas Creek as Teepee Flats, and shows Huckleberry Mountain at 5,355 feet. Hikers should spend time studying the old maps before attempting these explorations.

15 SULPHUR CREEK TRAIL

Distance: 3.2–4 miles round trip
Difficulty: Moderate
Type of trail: Occasionally maintained USFS trail
Starting point: 1,480 feet
High point: 2,100 feet
Elevation gain: 620 feet
Hikable: Spring, summer, fall
Maps: Green Trails No. 80 Cascade Pass; USGS Downey Mountain, Lime Mountain
Information: Darrington Ranger District, 360-436-1155
Cautions: Brush, blowdowns, river crossings, routefinding

Sulphur Creek Trail No. 793 is an old trail that begins from the end of the Suiattle River Road (Forest Road 26) and enters Glacier Peak Wilderness. *Tae Whatku* was the Sauk-Suiattle Indian name for the creek. The trail leads to Sulphur Hot Springs; many hikers have heard of Sulphur Hot Springs but may not know that the trail was once a route used by climbers to reach remote peaks such as Dome Peak. Twenty-year-old climbing guides report that the trail once extended more than 8 miles and was shown on 1939 maps. Most climbers who tackled this heavily vegetated valley vowed never to go back. The trail, originally built to intersect with the Pacific Crest Trail, was never completed, though it once continued for several miles on the south side of Sulphur Creek. Hikers with routefinding skills will enjoy the solitude, hot springs, and history of this area.

Though the hot springs are less than a mile from the trailhead, a ford of Sulphur Creek is involved. The crossing can be dangerous or impossible when rivers are running high. Hikers must ford or cross on precarious logs. Most hikers, including our party, have failed to locate the hot springs. Reports vary. Apparently the hot springs are not very hot as hot springs go (only about 80 degrees Fahrenheit). The hot springs are more difficult to locate in the melt-off when the springs lie underwater. If hot springs are your goal, Kennedy Hot Springs is in this district and easier to find.

Old-growth forest and the Wild and Scenic Suiattle River are truly the primary attractions of this trail. Some of the cedars along the last

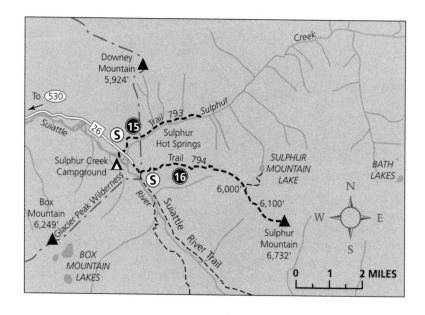

mile of maintained trail are 10 feet in girth, and the Douglas firs are not far behind. Early settlers often hiked up the valley just to see the old cedars. This is old-growth forest at its best; in May the forest is graced with calypso orchids, yellow violets, trilliums, bleeding heart, wild ginger, and false lily-of-the-valley. Devil's club reminds the hiker that Sulphur Creek is not Paradise.

From Interstate 5, drive State Route 530 east through Arlington and Darrington, then north to where it crosses the Sauk River. Just across the river where SR 530 continues north, turn east (right) onto Suiattle River Road (Forest Road 26). Drive 22 miles to the Sulphur Creek Campground and parking area. Park along the road unless you are spending the night at the campground.

The signed trail starts on the north side of the road (across from the campground) and enters Glacier Peak Wilderness in 0.5 mile. Just beyond the wilderness boundary, Glacier Peak can be seen. The trail drops to Sulphur Creek at 0.8 mile; the springs are on the other side of the creek at an elevation of 1,650 feet, but they are easier to smell than to find. In spring there is no safe way to cross the stream. The water will be high and the footlogs high above the water. There used to be a bridge, but it is long gone. We did find one piece of the bridge a short distance upstream from the logjam at this crossing. If the hot springs are your goal, come in late summer and cross the creek when water levels are low.

The trail is easy to follow another mile or so beyond the logjam. About 0.25 mile past the logjam, the trail crosses a boulder field. From the boulder field the trail can be followed for another 0.5 mile or so. However, the forest is reclaiming its territory and the trail becomes more difficult to follow with each passing year. Most hikers find the 1.6-mile trail challenging and rewarding, with many points of interest along the way. A couple of puncheon bridges remain in place, covered with moss, and several side paths descend to the river, leading to secluded viewpoints.

At about 1.6 miles, the semi-maintained trail is blocked by a large, fallen cedar, and most hikers turn around here. Only hikers with scrambling and routefinding skills should attempt to follow the old trail beyond this point. Persistent hikers who don't mind crawling over and under logs and squirming through blowdowns and tangles of brush can carry on another 0.5 mile or so. Beyond the fallen cedar, pieces of a very rough fishermen's path can be followed, but more downed trees and blowdowns make the going more difficult. If you get to a large boulder on the right-hand side of the path, you've probably gone about

Hikers face obstacles near the end of the Sulphur Creek Trail.

as far as anyone can go. Beyond the boulder, the terrain is a nightmare and there is no trace of a route.

16 SULPHUR MOUNTAIN TRAIL

Distance: 10 miles to viewpoint on ridge; 11 miles to summit
Difficulty: Challenging
Type of trail: Maintained USFS trail
Starting point: 1,800 feet
High point: 6,000 feet, viewpoint; 6,735 feet, summit
Elevation gain: 4,200 feet to viewpoint; 4,935 feet to summit
Hikable: Summer, fall
Maps: Green Trails No. 112 Glacier Peak; USGS Lime Mountain
Information: Darrington Ranger Station, 360-436-1155
Cautions: No water beyond creek at 0.25 mile
See Hike 15 for map

Sulphur Mountain Trail No. 794, a strenuous hike to lonesome country with great views, is often overlooked by hikers because it stays mostly in the forest and the views are near the end. The trail also provides access to the Bath Lakes High Route used by climbers. The Sulphur Mountain Trail becomes more interesting if you can obtain or borrow a copy of the out-of-print *Routes and Rocks* by Crowder and Tabor (The Mountaineers, 1965); the authors provide a geological background of the area as well as a detailed route description of the Bath Lakes High Route. Most everyone who hikes the Sulphur Mountain trail agrees on one thing—it is a "test your mettle" trail recommended for strong hikers. The trail starts steep and stays steep, with only a few level spots to catch your breath. You could call it Darrington's version of Mount Si. The only reliable water source is a small stream near the beginning of the hike (at about 2,200 feet), and in early August the stream is barely a trickle. Up to mid-July, you may be able to get water from snowmelt near the ridge crest, but don't count on it. Carry at least two quarts of water per person.

From Interstate 5 drive State Route 530 east through Arlington and Darrington, then north to where it crosses the Sauk River; just across the river where SR 530 continues north, turn east (right) onto Suiattle River Road (Forest Road 26). Drive 22.5 miles to the end of the road and parking beyond Sulphur Creek Campground. The trail begins on the Suiattle River Trail.

Hike a couple hundred yards on the Suiattle River Trail to the signed junction for Sulphur Mountain and take this trail to the left. It is in good condition as it climbs through salal and fir forest with a few mossy

A hazy view of Glacier Peak

boulders adding scenic touches here and there. There is very little undergrowth, but in summer you'll find coralroot (a member of the orchid family) and saprophytic plants, which live on dead and decaying vegetation. At 0.25 mile (about 2,200 feet), you'll see a small stream, the only water on this hike. The trail continues climbing relentlessly.

At about 3 miles (4,600 feet), the trail crosses a rocky bench and the steepness eases off a bit for the next 1.5 miles. At 4 miles the terrain changes as the trail traverses beneath a rock slide. Meadows alternate with forest, and hellebore and valerian line the trail. The trees are gradually left behind as the trail climbs the last mile through open country to the ridge crest and the first high point. As you attain the ridge crest at 5 miles (6,000 feet), the entire north face of Glacier Peak comes into view, filling the horizon. Far below is the Suiattle River valley, and above the valley Lime Ridge extends west from Glacier Peak. In early August the ridge crest is covered with flowers—western anemone, bistort, valerian, and lupine. Hopefully there is enough of a breeze to ward off the biting flies that often accompany such floral displays. Once you reach the ridge, there are options.

To descend to Sulphur Mountain Lake (5,189 feet), turn left and follow an obvious way trail. The lake is an excellent place to camp for those willing to carry a full pack up the trail and then down to the lake. Above Sulphur Mountain Lake to the northeast are Spire Point and Dome Peak, but you'll need the map to identify all the peaks.

For the true summit of Sulphur Mountain, continue following the main trail to the right, along the ridge crest, and enjoy the ever-expanding views. Looking back, you can see why Green Mountain is so named, but Glacier Peak to the south continues to steal the show. The Sauk-Suiattle tribes knew Glacier Peak as *Da Kobad*, which translates to "Great White Mother Mountain." The Sulphur Mountain summit involves a climb of 700 feet or so, and routefinding skills are required. From the second high point (6,100 feet), a way trail drops about 250 feet before climbing back to the ridge crest, but the trail is indistinct from that point. The summit is about 1 mile beyond. Fred Beckey, author of the *Cascade Alpine Guide* (The Mountaineers), writes that reaching the summit is "easy" (this may be taken with a grain of salt).

The Bath Lakes High Route begins high on Sulphur Mountain and traverses very rough country northeast 2.5 miles to Bath Lakes, ending at Canyon Lake. The route is a rigorous challenge; it climbs 3,600 feet and descends 4,500 feet, with many ups and downs. Only experienced climbers should attempt the entire route because a rope is needed for a steep section east of Bath Lakes.

17 TWENTY LAKES BASIN VIA IODINE GULCH

Distance: 6 miles round trip
Difficulty: Challenging
Type of trail: Maintained USFS way trail
Starting point: 2,600 feet
High point: 4,700 feet
Elevation gain: 2,100 feet
Hikable: Spring, summer, fall
Maps: Green Trails No. 109 Granite Falls, No. 110 Silverton
Information: Darrington Ranger Station, 360-436-1155
Cautions: Steep scramble

Twenty Lakes Basin in Mount Pilchuck State Park is known to some old-timers as "The Poor Man's Enchantments" and is known to others as Bathtub Lakes. The Green Trails maps do not reveal the many lakes

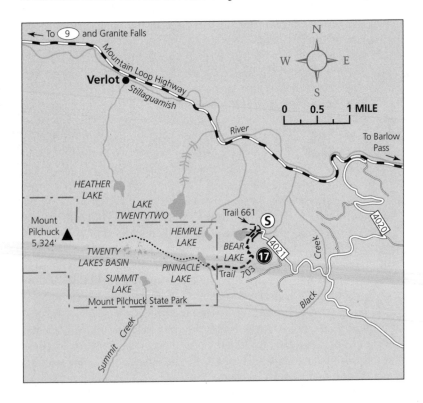

Mountain goat near Mount Pilchuck

and tarns that are nestled behind Mount Pilchuck, and most hikers who stop at Pinnacle Lake may not know about this enchanted, seldom-hiked area. Admittedly, we found more hikers on the route than we did seventeen years ago, but it's hard enough to get there that it is

unlikely to become overcrowded. The scattered tarns are barren of fish except for Summit Lake about 0.3 mile south of Bathtub Lakes.

From Interstate 5, drive east on US 2 to State Route 9 north and then SR 92 east to Granite Falls, where the road becomes the Mountain Loop Highway. Drive east on the Mountain Loop Highway past Verlot 4.5 miles to Schweitzer Road (Forest Road 4020) and turn right. Drive 2.6 miles, then turn right on Forest Road 4021 and continue 3.3 miles to the Pinnacle Lake Trailhead (Trail No. 703).

Hike the Pinnacle Lake Trail to the signed junction for Bear Lake in less than 0.05 mile; stay left. Continue on the Pinnacle Lake Trail as it climbs through magnificent old-growth forest and crosses Bear Creek on a bridge. As the trail switchbacks, look for an ancient cedar snag that towers over the trail and huge Douglas firs. In early September the Canadian dogwood is bright with berries and the ground is carpeted with false lily-of-the-valley. Parts of the trail are a patchwork of mud and slippery roots. As the trail levels off after about 1 mile, it passes small tarns; the trail is extremely muddy here and hikers have created bypasses—stay on the main trail if possible. Reach Pinnacle Lake (3,800 feet) at about 1.75 miles, a good place to take a break or call it a day. The lake may be far enough for hikers, but those with cross-country skills and stamina can continue on.

To reach Twenty Lakes Basin, hike clockwise on a faint path around the southwest side of Pinnacle Lake through grass and boulders. From the lake the route is a steep scramble through boulders, streams, grass, and vegetation. The path comes to a stream, then follows near and sometimes in the stream. In late summer the stream is shallow. Hiking poles come in handy here, especially on the descent. As the way trail climbs, Glacier Peak comes into view and Pinnacle Lake glints below. In late summer gentians are blue gems scattered through the grasses, and the whistle of a marmot may break the silence. When you get to Iodine Gulch (about 2,100 feet), you can't miss it. A large boulder marked with yellow paint reads "IODINE GULCH." A nearby boulder is painted with an arrow pointing downhill for the descent. Iodine Gulch is only the beginning of further exploration. Hikers with scrambling skills can follow the yellow daubs of paint to the scattered tarns of Twenty Lakes Basin (4,700 feet) at about 3 miles.

You can continue all the way to the summit ridge of Mount Pilchuck if you desire—it is about 4.5 miles one way from the Pinnacle Lake Trailhead to the summit of Mount Pilchuck (5,324 feet).

Twenty Lakes Basin

18 MARTEN CREEK TRAIL

Distance: 6.6 miles round trip to upper creek; 10.6 miles round trip to Granite Pass
Difficulty: Challenging
Type of trail: Occasionally maintained USFS trail
Starting point: 1,400 feet
High point: 2,700 feet, upper creek; 3,320 feet, Granite Pass
Elevation gain: 1,300 feet to upper creek; 1,920 feet to Granite Pass
Hikable: Spring, summer, fall (in winter, via snowshoes)
Maps: Green Trails No. 110 Silverton; USGS Silverton
Information: Darrington Ranger Station, 360-436-1155
Cautions: Brush, water on trail, routefinding

The Marten Creek Trail (Trail No. 713) is an old mining trail in the Boulder River Wilderness that climbed to Granite Pass and linked up with the Deer Creek Trail before it descended to Darrington via Clear Creek. It was the official trail between the Silverton Ranger Station and the Darrington Ranger District. The trail may have been named for an early prospector, S. J. Martin, one of the first miners to stake a claim in Silverton. Other prospectors found ore near the head of Marten Creek, and by 1896 there were more than forty mining claims in the area. A forest fire in 1897 burned the entire south slope of Long Mountain; it is believed the fire was caused by a spark from the Everett and Monte Cristo Railroad. By 1917 a trail ran up the east side of the creek.

In 1918 The Mountaineers chose Monte Cristo as the area for their annual outing. One of their destinations was a hike to Granite Pass. Margaret D. Hargrave wrote an account of the outing that was published in volume XI of *The Mountaineer:* "It was a hot, hot day, and after rounding Long Mountain and leaving the cooler shadows of Marten Creek, our trail simply evaporated. Did that give us pause? Not at all; we bucked brush, did some side-hill-nanny work, climbed a couple of waterfalls, crawled through more brush, and finally emerged at the foot of Granite Pass." After we hiked the trail recently, we can attest that this account could have been written yesterday. In 1925 a plantation reforestation project was established in which seedlings were taken from several areas and planted in the burned area. The trees have grown fast, crowding out the sky. Tags on the trees today

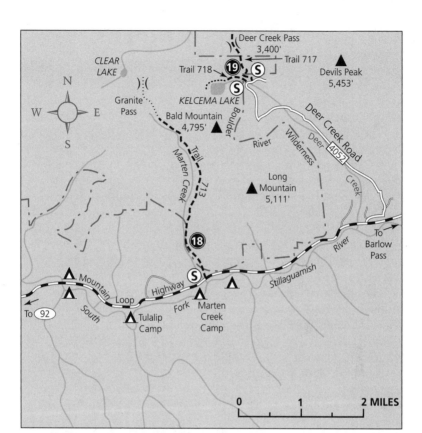

indicate their origin. By 1949 a road had been bulldozed up Marten Creek almost as far as Granite Pass.

This trail doesn't get a lot of use and so is a good example of a "hidden trail." Though the hike is mentioned in guidebooks, hikers usually drive past this trailhead to more popular hikes in the area. Marten Creek lacks the high drama of Mount Dickerman or Headlee Pass, and some hikers may find it an exasperating trail that starts out with purpose and then dies out in brush. There is no alpine lake at the end of it, nor a scenic summit from which a hiker can stand and peer across a sea of peaks. The summits that can be accessed from this trail are obscure and for technical climbers only. Even experienced climbers find themselves cursing the brush they must fight to reach Long Mountain (wise climbers wait until the brushy slopes of Long Mountain are snow-covered). Most hikers will be ready to stop at the upper reaches of Marten Creek, the end of the somewhat-maintained trail.

Beyond Marten Creek, the trail is obscure and best left to those with routefinding skills. Some parties have been able to follow the route to Granite Pass, but the trail is badly overgrown and difficult to follow. Rumors of the old trail persist—one on the east side, the other on the west side of the valley. Hikers who do get to the pass are rewarded with views to the north of Three Fingers, Big Bear, and Liberty Mountain.

In winter the Marten Creek Trail is a popular snowshoe trip because avalanche danger is not usually high. In spring when the snow melts out, sections of the trail become a virtual streambed, and as the trail approaches upper Marten Creek, it gets downright nasty. Wait for summer to make the best of this trail through old-growth forest.

From Interstate 5, drive east on US 2 to State Route 9 north and then SR 92 east to Granite Falls, where the road becomes the Mountain Loop Highway. Drive east on the Mountain Loop Highway past Verlot 9 miles, and just past Marten Creek Camp, look for a small parking area on the left side of the highway.

The first mile, a pleasant walk with occasional views to boulder fields through the trees, follows the road built in the 1940s to access mines. The trail enters the Boulder River Wilderness in 0.25 mile. In less than 0.5 mile, look for a large, greenish boulder (10 feet high) on which a tree is growing; in a little over 0.5 mile the route passes the tree plantation, designated with a signboard. Reports say that in recent years an old wood skid with iron tie bolts could be seen on the left side of the trail at just under 1 mile, but we did not see it. Charred stumps tell of the forest fire that swept down Long Mountain.

At 1.2 miles the trail crosses a stream and levels off as it enters the valley of Marten Creek, where the creek can now be seen and heard. At about 2.5 miles the trail enters a clearing of slide alder, and a little beyond is a view of Three Fingers. The trail continues through a stand of hemlock at 3 miles and crosses a stream before entering a marshy area and Marten Creek at 3.3 miles.

Experimental plot near the trailhead

The trail crosses the creek, then virtually disappears. The 1986 Green Trails map shows the maintained trail ending at a little over 3.5 miles at 2,700 feet. The original trail continued another 2 miles with 600 feet additional elevation gain to Granite Pass, 5.3 miles from the trailhead.

19 KELCEMA LAKE AND DEER CREEK PASS

Distance: 0.8 mile round trip to Kelcema Lake; 2 miles round trip to Deer Creek Pass
Difficulty: Moderate
Type of trail: Maintained/abandoned USFS trail
Starting point: 3,100 feet
High point: 3,182 feet, Kelcema Lake; 3,400 feet, Deer Creek Pass
Elevation gain: 82 feet to Kelcema Lake; 300 feet to Deer Creek Pass
Hikable: Summer, fall (snowshoe/ski in winter)
Map: Green Trails No. 110 Silverton
Information: Darrington Ranger District, 360-436-1155
Cautions: Brush, routefinding
See Hike 18 for map

The access road to Kelcema Lake begins at Deer Creek, a popular winter recreation area in Mount Baker–Snoqualmie National Forest. The beginning of the Deer Creek Road was a railroad stop for the Everett and Monte Cristo Railroad, for the Bonanza Queen Mine located upstream on Deer Creek. There is a lot of history packed into this tiny lake in the Boulder River Wilderness beneath Bald Mountain, which was first climbed in 1897 by Louis Fletcher. Originally the lake was called Deer Lake, then renamed Kehama but due to an error was changed to Kelcema, and it has remained Kelcema ever since. It still shows as Lake Kehama on the 1917 Snoqualmie National Forest map. In the late 1800s a mining camp was located below the lake, with more than forty claims along Deer Creek. A wagon road climbed the east side of Deer Creek and continued to Deer Creek Pass. The Clear Creek Trail from Darrington to Deer Creek Pass was a shortcut between Verlot and Darrington used by the Forest Service. The other remaining piece of the original trail is the Frog Lake Trail, which takes off from the south end of the Clear Creek Campground. Purists can seek out other fragments of the trail, but road building and logging have destroyed most of it.

Ancient cedar near Deer Creek Pass

In the 1920s Kelcema Lake was the site of a Boy Scout summer camp. Virgil Peterson enjoyed the Monte Cristo area as a young man and climbed many of the region's peaks. He remembers the Boy Scout camp and gave this account in a personal letter: "The Boy Scout camp at Lake Kelcema was located right where Deer Creek emerges from the lake. I was there for ten days in 1931. It hosted many young men from around Snohomish County, the most notable of whom was Henry M. 'Scoop' Jackson, U.S. Senate." He also recalled "an overnight hike over Deer Creek Pass and down Clear Creek to the point that one of its main tributaries, Copper Creek, showed up, and then up Copper Creek to the remains of the old Bornite mine. It shipped ore on a tramway to where Clear Creek joined the Sauk River." Virgil was often given the assignment of hiking down to Silverton to fetch the mail. Today Kelcema Lake is a good destination for the family and beginning hikers. In winter it is a good snowshoe or ski trip, but it's a challenge because the trip begins from the start of the Deer Creek Road—it is 1,500 feet elevation gain and about 8 miles round trip from the beginning of the road to the lake. The poorly maintained trail to Deer Creek Pass is not in a wilderness area; though the hike is short, it is not suitable for children because the trail consists of slippery puncheon, brush, and downed trees. Beyond Deer Creek Pass, routefinding and scrambling skills are required.

From Interstate 5, drive east on US 2 to State Route 9 north and then SR 92 east to Granite Falls, where the road becomes the Mountain Loop Highway. Drive east on the Mountain Loop Highway past Verlot and Marten Creek Camp to Deer Creek Road (Forest Road 4052) at milepost 23. Turn left and drive 1 mile to a junction. Stay left on Forest Road 4052 and drive 3.5 miles to the signed trailhead for Trail No. 718. Devils Thumb, just north of Devils Peak, can be seen from the parking lot. There are no facilities.

The trail is short, well graded, and easy to follow. At 0.4 mile reach Kelcema Lake, with an outhouse and campsites. On the north side of the lake, a large boulder makes a pleasant promontory on which to picnic; it also serves as a jumping-off point for youngsters on a hot summer day. In late summer, lily pads bloom on the lake and Canadian dogwood may be showing bright red berries. Hikers can explore a rough trail that goes around the north side of the lake counterclockwise to a talus slope with a hint of a mysterious trail beyond. There is a good view of Devils Peak and Devils Thumb from this end of the lake.

For hikers who want to explore Deer Creek Pass too, the trailhead for Trail No. 717 is a short distance up the road from the Kelcema Lake trailhead. The forested trail with slippery puncheon, brush, and blowdowns leads in about 1 mile to Deer Creek Pass, with views of Three Fingers, Liberty, and Whitehorse. A few ancient cedar trees grow near the pass. Don't expect high drama—the pass is a quiet spot tucked away in remnants of old-growth forest.

From the pass, the brushy trail descends roughly 0.5 mile to meet the Clear Creek Road (3,000 feet). Strong hikers may want to hike the trail one way, which involves a time-consuming car shuttle, but check with the Darrington Ranger District because the Clear Creek Road may not be drivable to its end. In 2000 the last few miles of the road were being considered for closure by the Forest Service. Even if the road is open, the final 2 miles of the Clear Creek Road are extremely rough, and even a four-wheel-drive vehicle will be challenged.

A trail once led northeast from Deer Creek Pass to a cabin and mines on Helena Peak, but the trail is now very faint. Hikers have found the very rough and hazardous trail and hiked it recently; those with climbing skills may welcome this opportunity to explore seldom-climbed Helena Peak, riddled with old mines, cabin sites, and artifacts dating back to the 1890s.

20 DOUBLE EAGLE MINE AND DEVILS LAKES

> **Distance: 5.4 miles round trip to mine; 6 miles round trip to lakes**
> **Difficulty:** Extremely challenging
> **Type of trail:** Abandoned road/cross-country route
> **Starting point:** 1,968 feet
> **High point:** 3,650 feet, mine; 3,800 feet, lakes
> **Elevation gain:** 1,682 feet to mine; 1,832 feet to lakes
> **Hikable:** Summer, fall
> **Maps:** Green Trails No. 110 Silverton; USGS Silverton
> **Information:** Darrington Ranger Station, 360-436-1155
> **Cautions:** Brush, routefinding

The Deer Creek area in Mount Baker–Snoqualmie National Forest was once an active mining area in the Monte Cristo district. The Deer Creek Road leads to several interesting sites, including Deer Creek Pass and Kelcema Lake (Hike 19). Lesser-known points of interest are Double Eagle Mine and Devils Lakes, which can be reached by an old road and abandoned trail by hikers with navigational skills. The road (sometimes referred to as Double Eagle Road in old trail guides) is not drivable, but

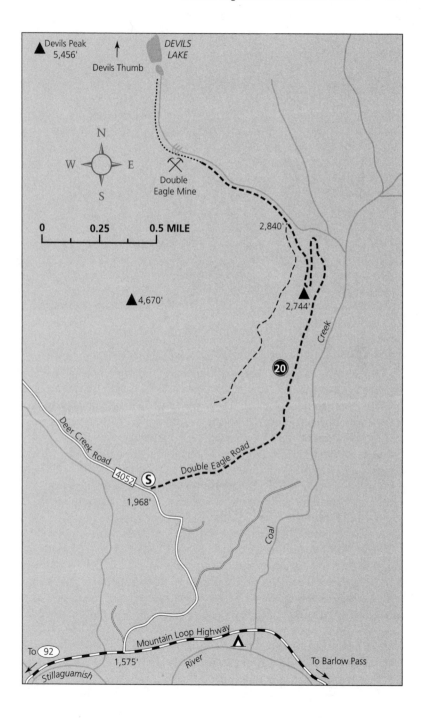

A hiker peers into one of the Double Eagle Mines.

can be walked to its end, where a rough trail takes off to the lakes. Save the mine, waterfall, and lakes until summer to enjoy the area's history and solitude. This old road also makes a good snowshoe trip in the winter, offering solitude because most snowshoers and skiers are bound for popular Kelcema Lake. This is one of the more challenging hikes in this guide. Double Eagle Mine and a spectacular waterfall at 3 miles are enough of a destination for most hikers, but scramblers can continue beyond the falls to Devils Lakes, which are set between Devils Peak and Devils Thumb north of Silverton. The lakes, though they are on national forest land, are not described in hiking guides and do not show on the Green Trails maps, but do show on the 7.5-minute USGS Silverton map. Leaf fossils have been found along this road.

From Interstate 5, drive east on US 2 to State Route 9 north and then SR 92 east to Granite Falls, where the road becomes the Mountain Loop Highway. Drive east on the Mountain Loop Highway past Verlot and Marten Creek Camp to Deer Creek Road (Forest Road 4052) at milepost 23. Turn left and drive 1 mile to a junction; here look for an overgrown road going off to the right, and park.

The route follows the west side of Coal Creek all the way to Devils Lake. It begins on the unsigned Double Eagle Road. The road switchbacks three times. At 1.5 miles reach the first switchback; from here it is possible to climb cross-country next to the creek less than 0.25 mile and intersect the trail at the third switchback, but it is easier just to follow the road because it is becoming more trail-like with each passing year. At about 1.8 miles reach the second switchback (2,744 feet).

At about 2.1 miles reach the third switchback (2,840 feet), where there is a junction. The main road is bermed and continues straight ahead; make a sharp turn to the right on an even more overgrown road. This section of road is rapidly becoming overgrown, but can still be followed. At about 2.4 miles, cross a creek (about 3,200 feet), then follow flags and old trail. Here it is fairly easy to stay on the trail, as only a couple of sections are truly indistinct. Stick close to the trail if you can, to avoid huckleberry brush and devil's club. The trail follows near the creek to the Double Eagle Mine at about 2.7 miles and the end of the trail. Apparently there are two mines, but we found only the one located at the base of a waterfall. The mine is on the left side of the waterfall that comes from a creek that flows from Devils Lakes basin.

If the lakes are your objective, traverse left from the mine through open areas and then north to a basin between Devils Peak and Devils Thumb. Once you reach the basin, faint trails lead to the lakes and potential campsites at about 3 miles.

From the lakes, Devils Peak (5,456 feet) can be scrambled and is sometimes done as a winter climb by experienced climbers.

21 OLD GOVERNMENT TRAIL

Distance: 4 miles round trip to waterfall; 6 miles round trip to Buck Creek
Difficulty: Moderate
Type of trail: Maintained USFS trail
Starting point: 2,361 feet
High point: 2,660 feet
Elevation gain: 300 feet
Hikable: Spring, summer, fall
Maps: Green Trails No. 111 Sloan Peak; USGS Bedal
Information: Darrington Ranger Station, 360-436-1155
Cautions: Brush, old puncheon, routefinding

Most hikers have probably never heard of the Old Government Trail, a quiet little trail in Mount Baker–Snoqualmie National Forest that

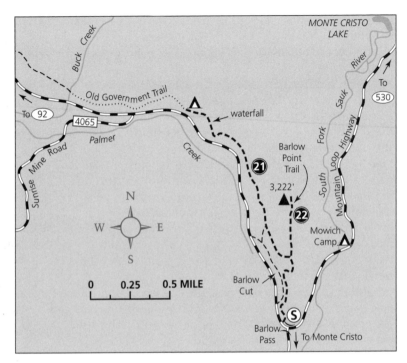

parallels the Mountain Loop Highway and does not get a lot of attention in guidebooks. The trail, built in 1917, is part of an old trail system that once ran from the mining community of Silverton to Barlow Pass. This low mountain pass between the Stillaguamish and Sauk watersheds was named for J. P. Barlow, a railroad surveyor who worked in the area in 1891. Today's trailhead parking lot is on the site of the Barlow Pass Guard Station (1917–1949). Barlow Cut, a section of the Hartford Eastern Railway (Everett and Monte Cristo Railroad), can be found a short distance from the Barlow Point/Old Government Trailhead. The combination of flooding and dwindling mining activity led to the discontinuation of the railroad in 1935. In 1936 the iron rails and wood ties were dismantled by a CCC crew as they constructed the Mountain Loop Highway.

On the 1966 USGS Bedal map, the Old Government Trail is shown going all the way from Barlow Pass to Silverton; on the Green Trails map, it is shown ending at about 2 miles. Though the trail is official

The waterfall at the end of the Old Government Trail

Historic photo of the Barlow Point Guard Station
Photo courtesy of Virgil Peterson

and the trailhead is signed, it is not a prominent trail with a dramatic conclusion, and by the time Barlow Pass is snowfree, most hikers are heading for higher elevations. But the Old Government Trail offers solitude and railroad history. The first 2 miles are an easy walk as the trail winds through deep forest with occasional glimpses down to the old railroad grade. The Forest Service maintains the trail, but old sections of slippery puncheon remain. The silent forest is studded with erratic boulders, and charred trees tell the story of old fires: Buck Creek and the slopes of Mount Dickerman were the scene of several forest fires in the late 1800s/early 1900s. The trail crosses a few small streams and at approximately 2 miles comes to a waterfall, the most scenic feature of the trail. This is a pretty place to stop; if you sit still long enough, you might get a glimpse of a mink that lives near the waterfall. It might be possible to continue on to Buck Creek, one of the sites where The Mountaineers camped in the early 1900s on their Annual Summer Outing.

From Interstate 5, drive east on US 2 to State Route 9 north and then SR 92 east to Granite Falls, where the road becomes the Mountain

Loop Highway. Drive east on the Mountain Loop Highway past Verlot to Barlow Pass, 30.6 miles east of Granite Falls. Park in the main parking lot off the highway, and look for the signed trailhead near the parking area and restroom. The Old Government Trail and Barlow Point Trail (Hike 22) start from the same parking area.

Start from the parking area and follow the Barlow Point Trail. The trail parallels the Barlow Cut for about 0.4 mile, then switchbacks up 0.3 mile to the high point of the trail at the signed junction for the Old Government Trail at about 0.7 mile. The Barlow Point Trail leads to the right; go left on the Old Government Trail. The trail then loses most of the elevation gain, contouring at 2,400 feet for 0.4 mile, then dropping a bit more to contour through forest.

For a variation at the start, a short distance from the trailhead turn left (toward the highway) at an unsigned trail junction. This unsigned trail leads to the Barlow Cut, a remnant of the Everett and Monte Cristo railroad grade. A placard gives the history of this historic spot, but the site is unkempt and overgrown. The railroad grade can be hiked about 0.5 mile and in spring makes a lovely walk. Though the railroad grade soon dies out, experienced hikers can find an unsigned trail heading uphill that intersects the Old Government Trail. Or you can continue to the end of the railroad grade, then climb cross-country to meet the Old Government Trail at about its 1-mile point. The forest is open here and the Old Government Trail is easy to spot.

The Old Government Trail crosses several small streams before it comes to the waterfall at about 2 miles. The trail continues from the waterfall a short distance before descending to apparently the end of the maintained trail at an area where people car-camp. We've heard that the trail continues beyond this point, but our attempts to locate the trail were unsuccessful. From the car-camping spot, the very faint trail soon dies out.

If you lose the trail at the car-camping area, you can hike cross-country to Buck Creek (leave a car at Buck Creek to hike the trail one way). It is about another mile to Buck Creek. Only hikers with cross-country hiking and navigation skills should continue from the car-camping spot to Buck Creek. If you get to Buck Creek, it is a short descent to the highway and you don't have to ford the creek.

Another variation is to leave a second car at the Sunrise Mine Road 4065 (milepost 28.1 on the Mountain Loop Highway). Start from the Barlow Point Trailhead, follow the Old Government Trail (or Barlow Cut variation) to the car-camping spot, and continue beyond the car-camping area toward Buck Creek until you see the Sunrise Mine Road and descend to the road. The road is easily spotted through the trees about midway between the car-camping area and Buck Creek. This shortens the hike by about 0.4 mile one way.

22 BARLOW POINT TRAIL

Distance: 2.5 miles round trip
Difficulty: Moderate
Type of trail: Maintained USFS trail
Starting point: 2,361 feet
High point: 3,222 feet
Elevation gain: 861 feet
Hikable: Spring, summer, fall
Maps: Green Trails No. 111 Sloan Peak; USGS Bedal
Information: Darrington Ranger Station, 360-436-1155
Cautions: None
See Hike 21 for map

Barlow Point Trail No. 709 is another short hike in the Barlow Pass area that can easily be added to the Old Government Trail (Hike 21). The Barlow Point Trail was built in 1935–36 by the Forest Service, and a lookout house was constructed on the summit. The lookout was destroyed in 1965. From the summit there are good views to the south of Silvertip, Lewis, and National Peaks.

From Interstate 5, drive east on US 2 to State Route 9 north and then SR 92 east to Granite Falls, where the road becomes the Mountain Loop Highway. Drive east on the Mountain Loop Highway past Verlot to Barlow Pass, 30.6 miles east of Granite Falls. Park in the main parking lot off the highway, and look for the signed trailhead near the parking area and restroom. The Barlow Point Trail and Old Government Trail start from the same parking area.

Follow the Barlow Point Trail as it parallels the Barlow Cut for about 0.4 mile, then switchbacks up 0.3 mile to the signed junction at about 0.7 mile. The Old Government Trail leads to the left; go right to continue on the Barlow Point Trail. The trail makes several switchbacks to the crest of the ridge. This ridge was also burned by the Buck Creek fire early in the twentieth century (see Hike 21). Near the summit you can often find brilliant clumps of penstemon in rocky outcroppings.

Penstemon

The trail then climbs another 0.5 mile or so to the summit of Barlow Point (3,222 feet), the site of the Barlow Point Lookout.

23 STILLAGUAMISH MEADOWS

Distance: 8 miles round trip
Difficulty: Challenging
Type of trail: Maintained USFS way trail
Starting point: 2,100 feet
High point: 5,200 feet
Elevation gain: 2,900 feet
Hikable: Summer, fall
Maps: Green Trails No. 111 Sloan Peak, No. 110 Silverton
Information: Darrington Ranger District, 360-436-1155
Cautions: Stillaguamish Peak considered a scramble—
hikers should not attempt the summit; avalanche
danger in the spring

The path that leads to the base of Stillaguamish Peak in Mount Baker–Snoqualmie National Forest is a textbook example of a way trail created by hikers and climbers. So many hikers have used this route that it is almost a "real" trail most of the way. The Perry Creek valley is extremely prone to avalanche early in the season; make sure the snow is gone before hiking into this valley. In summer it is a rocky trail that is hard on the feet. The base of the peak is a satisfying enough destination for most; strong, experienced hikers with trailfinding skills shouldn't have a problem, but save this exploration for good weather. The views are the major attraction.

From Interstate 5, drive east on US 2 to State Route 9 north and then SR 92 east to Granite Falls, where the road becomes the Mountain Loop Highway. Drive east on the Mountain Loop Highway, pass Verlot, and continue 15.5 miles farther. Turn left on Perry Creek Road No. 4063 and drive 1 mile to the end of the road and the trailhead.

The Perry Creek Trail No. 711 begins by traversing through forest, then curves to the right to contour beneath Mount Dickerman. The trail becomes a combination of vegetation and rubble as it contours above Perry Creek. The trail crosses talus fields, several streams, and dense pockets of vegetation before descending to Perry Creek Falls at 1.9 miles. Cross Perry Creek, which can be dangerous if the stream level is high. Continue as the trail climbs steeply through forest before

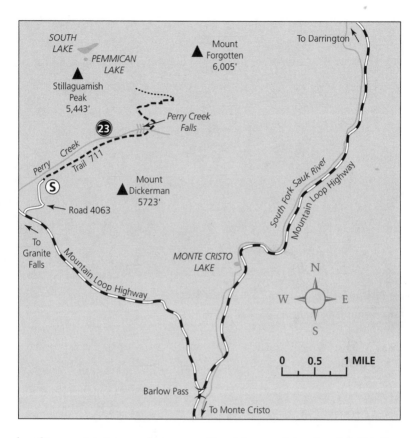

breaking out into meadows near the ridge crest in about 1.5 miles from Perry Creek Falls (about 3.5 miles from the trailhead). Paths seem to go everywhere, but the main trail continues to the right to Mount Forgotten Meadows; this is the beginning of the climbers' route to Mount Forgotten.

Continue straight on a path to a saddle on the ridge and turn left toward Stillaguamish Peak on an unmarked way trail that follows along and near the crest of the ridge. The trail comes to a rocky outcropping and you lose a bit of elevation here as the trail avoids it. The trail returns to the ridge crest and continues contouring through shrubs and flowers, breaking out into open meadows and rock gardens. Stillaguamish Peak, 5,443 feet, and Mount Forgotten, 6,005 feet, come into view. Follow the trail to a steep gully on the crest of the ridge near the base of Stillaguamish Peak. This is the obvious end of the trail, and hikers should content themselves with the view of South Lake below

Hikers approach Stillaguamish Peak

and the surrounding peaks. It is about 0.5 mile from the crest of the ridge to the base of Stillaguamish Peak.

24 BEDAL BASIN/BEDAL CREEK TRAIL

Distance: 4.8 miles round trip
Difficulty: Challenging
Type of trail: Occasionally maintained USFS trail
Starting point: 2,800 feet
High point: 5,000 feet
Elevation gain: 2,200 feet
Hikable: Summer, fall
Maps: Green Trails No. 111 Sloan Peak; USGS Bedal, Sloan
   Peak
Information: Darrington Ranger District, 360-436-1155
Cautions: Brush, stream crossings, routefinding

If you hike the Bedal Basin (also called Bedal Creek) Trail into the valley beneath Sloan Peak in the Henry M. Jackson Wilderness, you may find the remains of a trapper's cabin built in 1931–1933 by Harry Bedal, a legendary mountain man best known for overseeing the construction of the Three Fingers lookout. He worked as the trail foreman for Harold Engles, Darrington District Ranger. In 1929 Engles and Bedal scouted out Three Fingers as a potential lookout site and got to within 15 feet of the summit before being turned back by snow. There was no trail—the district was still largely unexplored and only sketchily mapped. Crashing through the brush cross-country to have a look at a remote mountain was just a typical day's work. Bedal was notorious for being tight-lipped. Keith Markwell, who has hiked and climbed in the area, didn't know Bedal personally but did know Harold Engles. In a personal letter, Markwell wrote, "Harold told of the time when he was returning from the Kennedy–Lake Byrne area and met Harry at Crystal Creek. Harry had finished his work there and also his breakfast, so he

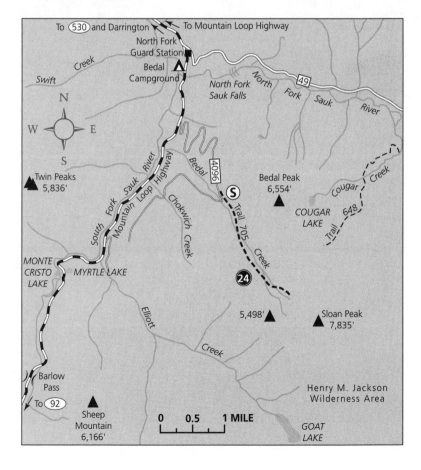

The remains of Harry Bedal's cabin

suggested they hike out to Darrington together. 'Are you about ready, Harry?' [asked Harold]. 'Just pee on the fire and call the dog,' said Harry, and never spoke another word during the 20-mile hike out."

The Bedal family homesteaded on the Sauk River. Bedal's mother was the daughter of a Suiattle chief, and Harry was born at Sauk Prairie in 1890. Harry and his sisters, Edith and Jean, acquired outdoor skills as youngsters. The family had an asbestos claim high on Sloan Peak called the Phoenix. Harry built a trail to the mine and later constructed the cabin, but the mine never panned out. Bedal Creek was named for Harry's father, James, in the late 1890s—the Sauk Indians called the creek *Chich-chetku*. The cabin is gone now, but a few foundation timbers remain along with a few rusting cans and shards of broken glass. The upper valley where the cabin stood was called Goat Pasture long ago and is a wild and lonesome spot, set between giant boulders and clumps of subalpine trees. A small stream runs through it, and in late summer purple and yellow monkey flowers nod in the breeze. Sloan Peak dominates the horizon but other peaks can be seen, including Mount Pugh, White Chuck Mountain, and Bedal Peak (6,554 feet). Sloan Peak, named for James Sloan, a prospector of the 1890s, was first climbed in 1921.

The Forest Service had established the trail by 1921–26. The trail climbed the north side of Bedal Creek from what we know today as the Mountain Loop Highway. Near the end of the Bedal Creek Trail, another trail once branched left at about 4,000 feet and climbed partway to the saddle between Sloan and Bedal Peaks. The trail to the saddle would have joined Sloan Creek Trail No. 648 (Cougar Creek Trail), but the trail was never completed. On the USGS Sloan Peak map, the Cougar Creek Trail is shown climbing to 4,800 feet and the Bedal Basin Trail climbing to 4,440 feet. In 1990 the Bedal Basin Trail, now in the Henry M. Jackson Wilderness, was in poor condition and almost impossible to follow. The salmonberries were head-high, and only a few strategically placed flags helped guide the way to the basin. In some sections there was no trail at all, and part of the route consisted of hiking up the streambed. A few attempts have been made recently to clear the brush, but the Forest Service admits this is a low-priority trail. In late August, even when the sun is shining the brush may be so wet from dew that hikers are soaked by the time they hike through the first pocket of brush. Hikers with routefinding skills nonetheless enjoy visiting this historical site, with its views of Sloan Peak and its solitude.

From Interstate 5, drive east on US 2 to State Route 9 north and then SR 92 east to Granite Falls, where the road becomes the Mountain Loop Highway. Drive east on the Mountain Loop Highway 30.6 miles to

Barlow Pass, and continue north on the Mountain Loop Highway. It crosses Bedal Creek at about 6 miles; this was likely the location of the original trail. At about 6.5 miles from Barlow Pass, turn right on Forest Road 4096. You can also approach from Darrington: From Interstate 5, drive east on State Route 530 through Arlington to Darrington, then south on the Mountain Loop Highway 17 miles to the North Fork Sauk River bridge, and about 0.5 mile beyond the bridge turn left on Forest Road 4096. From either approach, continue 3 rough miles to the end of the road. The trailhead sign may or may not be there, but you can see the trail heading steeply uphill.

The 1938 Stillaguamish-Sauk-Suiattle Recreational Areas map (Mount Baker National Forest) shows the old trail beginning from the road and climbing beside Bedal Creek. Today the trail alternates between avalanche paths and pockets of ancient forest, leveling off a bit as it approaches Bedal Creek at about 0.5 mile. Old hiking guides describe a campsite at the creek and crossing the creek (on a log). The campsite has apparently washed away after several winters, and the route has changed. Just before the trail approaches the creek, look for an unmarked trail junction where the right-hand branch leads down to the creek and the crossing where the log used to be; stay straight.

There are several downed trees on the trail. The trail crosses a stream—many small streams are crossed along the trail—and returns to the forest before a major crossing of Bedal Creek at about 1.2 miles (3,400 feet). The trail then returns to the forest again, then parallels Bedal Creek before vanishing altogether into the streambed at about 1.7 miles (3,800 feet). This may have been where the partially completed trail to Cougar Creek climbed toward the Sloan-Bedal saddle. This important junction is marked with double cairns that are all too easy to miss on the descent.

From here the route consists of finding your way up the streambed or beside it, depending on conditions. Once you leave the woods, climb about 200 feet and look for the trail heading off into the forest on the right-hand side of the stream. The trail then climbs steeply through forest and ends at about 2.4 miles at the lip of the basin (about 5,000 feet) beneath Sloan Peak where Bedal's cabin once stood. From the meadow, hikers can scramble to Point 5498 on the ridge for views down to Goat Lake and the west face of Sloan Peak.

On your way back, watch carefully for a split in the stream that you may not have noticed on your ascent. Avoid the branch to the left and follow the right-hand branch of the creek downhill until you come to the double cairns. If you miss the cairns, backtrack until you find them again. It is easy to miss this turnoff, especially when you are distracted by the view of Mount Baker through the trees.

25 RED MOUNTAIN LOOKOUT

Distance: 2 miles round trip
Difficulty: Moderate
Type of trail: Maintained/abandoned USFS trail
Starting point: 2,100 feet
High point: 2,800 feet
Elevation gain: 700 feet
Hikable: Summer, fall
Maps: Green Trails No. 111 Sloan Peak; USGS Sloan Peak
Information: Darrington Ranger District, 360-436-1155
Cautions: Rock-scrambling, routefinding above lookout site

This short and scenic trail in Mount Baker–Snoqualmie National Forest leads to the Red Mountain lookout site; the lookout was built in 1936 and removed in 1967. Although the trail to the lookout site (Trail No. 657) is only 1 mile, the journey is spectacular. Once the trail leaves the North Fork Sauk Trail, it climbs through ancient forest of huge cedars, firs, and pockets of vine maple. The trail to the lookout site is in good condition, but is not prominently featured in hiking guides and is often overlooked by hikers. The trail may be too short to satisfy some hikers, though they can easily combine it with another trail in the area. Hikers and scramblers enjoy views of Sloan Peak, Pride Basin, and Mount Pugh. Experienced mountaineers can continue 4 miles on from the lookout site to explore an abandoned trail that continues to Ruby Lake (5,439 feet) or the summit of Red Mountain (6,975 feet).

Whether your destination is the lookout site, Ruby Lake, or Red Mountain, the highlight of the trail is the views. From the lookout site, the views of Sloan Peak (7,835 feet), sometimes referred to as the Matterhorn of the Cascades, are breathtaking. According to Fred Beckey in the *Cascade Alpine Guide* (The Mountaineers Books, 1973), the Indian name for Red Mountain was *Ska-hala-bats*, which means "Painted Mountain." Incredibly, Sloan Peak was first climbed by non-mountaineers using boots with caulks on the glacier—the climbers did not even have ice axes.

From Interstate 5, drive east on US 2 to State Route 9 north and then SR 92 east to Granite Falls, where the road becomes the Mountain

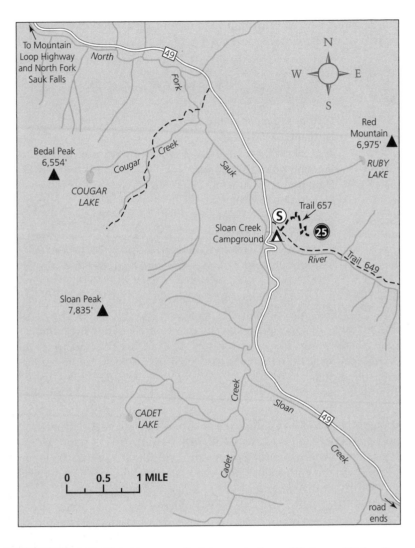

Loop Highway. Drive east on the Mountain Loop Highway 30.6 miles to Barlow Pass and continue north on the Mountain Loop Highway about 8 miles, then turn right on Forest Road 49 (Sloan Creek Road). You can also approach from Darrington: From Interstate 5, drive east on State Route 530 through Arlington to Darrington, then south on the Mountain Loop Highway 19 miles to Forest Road 49 (Sloan Creek Road) and turn left. From either approach, follow the road 7 miles to the Sloan Creek Campground and parking area. There are facilities.

Begin on North Fork Sauk Trail No. 649. Hike a couple hundred yards to the junction with the Red Mountain Trail (Trail No. 657) and turn left. The trail begins to climb through old-growth forest and continues to an open spot where the lookout used to be at about 1 mile. The structure is gone but the views are still here—to the south is Pride Basin and the Cadets, but Sloan Peak steals the show. Hikers are advised to stop here; the trail continues on from the lookout site for approximately 4 miles, but is rough, steep, and not maintained.

From the lookout site, the trail climbs 300 feet to a rocky outcropping. The trail is easy to follow to this point, but only hikers with rock-scrambling skills should attempt to follow the route beyond. Climbers and hikers with scrambling skills may be able to negotiate the rocky outcropping and follow a way trail, but we did not get beyond the outcropping.

Hikers who don't have the skills to explore beyond the rocky outcropping can enjoy other destinations along Sloan Creek Road, such as the short trail leading to North Fork Sauk Falls. The well-signed

Sloan Peak from the trail to the Red Mountain lookout

trailhead is about a mile from the Mountain Loop Highway, or about 5 miles northwest of the Red Mountain Trailhead. The trail to the falls, Trail No. 660, is less than a quarter-mile in length. See the map for Hike 24, Bedal Basin/Bedal Creek Trail.

The lowlands come to life, North Cascades

US HIGHWAY 2/
STEVENS PASS

26 LAKE ISABEL

Distance: 7.5 miles round trip
Difficulty: Extremely challenging
Type of trail: Old roads/scramble route
Starting point: 400 feet
High point: 2,847 feet
Elevation gain: Approximately 2,450 feet
Hikable: Spring, summer, fall
Maps: USFS, Skykomish Ranger District (1991)
Information: Skykomish Ranger District, 360-677-2414
Cautions: Difficult routefinding, stream crossings, unsigned junctions

Lake Isabel is elusive, lying at the edge of the Ragged Ridge Roadless Area; it is not easy to get to, but hikers with scrambling skills who persevere find much to satisfy them on this extremely challenging route. Routefinding skills are essential. There are good reasons the hike is not described in many guidebooks. The upper trail is rough, and getting to the lake involves a scramble. The trail has many unmarked

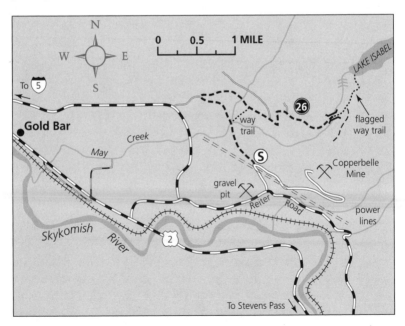

junctions that may baffle even the most experienced routefinders. New roads and motorbike trails do not all show on the maps, which adds to the confusion. You cannot totally rely on the map for guidance, though the USGS Index map shows more of the road system. Allow extra time and the flexibility to turn back if necessary. People have gotten lost here. This hike is not recommended for most hikers.

You probably will not have the entire trail to yourself—it is a multi-use trail, and hikers must share a good section of the route with motorcycles and ATVs, so be respectful of other users along the way. Hikers find the way to Lake Isabel an odd blend of ugliness and beauty, a trail of extremes. How else to describe a hike that begins from motorcycle staging pits and leads to a remote lake that most hikers never see? Reserve a weekday to explore this area that has mining history, waterfalls, and Lake Isabel. Apparently there was a resort at the lake long ago.

The Copperbelle Mine, one of the most significant mines in the Index area, dates back to 1897. Later it became known as the Bunker Hill Mine. There was a concentrator near the main tunnel. A smelter was connected to the concentrator by a flume. There were other structures associated with the mines, but most of these artifacts are gone. If you do come across mines in your exploration, do not enter them because many mines contain winzes (vertical mine shafts) of unknown depth that are sometimes flooded. On our latest visit, we learned that the Copperbelle Mine is no longer accessible to the public. A new logging road with a gate has closed the route to the mine. We came across the mine but were greeted by watchmen near the gate. Do not attempt to hike to the Copperbelle Mine because it is now private property.

Drive US 2 east to Gold Bar and go about 1.5 miles beyond to Reiter Road. Turn left and drive 2 miles to a major staging area for motorcyclists and off-road vehicles. Just past the gravel pit on the left at 2 miles, turn left on a newly graveled road and go about 0.3 mile (northwest), under the power lines, to a parking area just before a T intersection. The hike begins from this parking area and avoids private property and gated roads.

From the parking area, walk a short distance away from the power lines to the T intersection. Turn left onto a dirt road with mud puddles and potholes. Follow the road to the left (north) as it turns toward May Creek. Several bike paths lead off from this road, but stay on the road until in 0.6 mile you come out at May Creek and a log to scoot across on. If you don't find the log, you've taken a side road; go back and try again. After crossing the log, walk upstream to rejoin the road at a Y intersection (to the right is a very steep way trail). Go to the left, uphill, on an obvious trail used by hikers and occasional motorcycles 0.5 mile to approximately 820 feet, where you come out on a main road at a T intersection at about 1 mile (to the left the road goes west to Gold Bar). Turn right and continue on this road. It crosses the stream several times (in June the crossings were not difficult), but generally the road deteriorates as it climbs.

At another junction at about 2 miles (just below 1,200 feet), stay left. The road is very rocky here and at about 3 miles you come to a wooden road bridge that is deteriorating but still used by hikers and jeeps. This is a good spot to take a break. Climb a bit more and at 2,120 feet you come to a bulldozed area. Ignore the fresh jeep track heading toward a waterfall and stay on the road until you see another road remnant that climbs into a forested section. Be careful here—it is vague. The road remnant leads to a flagged way trail on your left at about 2,260 feet. This trail gets you to the lake.

Along the way the trail passes a waterfall at about 3.75 miles (2,800 feet). Sections of old puncheon are found here, pockets of old growth, and amazingly large cedars. From the waterfall a scramble route climbs

Lake Isabel

a short way to the lake. Generally if you keep heading uphill and stay near May Creek, you'll probably get there.

The lake is lovely, but the primitive campsites around the lake are strewn with garbage. For a pristine lunch spot with a view of the lake and Ragged Ridge, cross the lake outlet on a logjam and find a place to sit.

27 MINERAL CITY/SILVER CREEK

Distance: 6 miles round trip
Difficulty: Moderate
Type of trail: Old road/miners' trail
Starting point: 1,100 feet
High point: 1,750 feet
Elevation gain: 650 feet
Hikable: Summer, fall
Map: Green Trails No. 143 Monte Cristo
Information: Skykomish Ranger District, 360-677-2414
Cautions: Stream crossings, rock slide, brush and routefinding beyond Mineral City

This trail is described in other hiking guides and magazines, but all hikers need to discover it. This is by far one of the most beautiful places we have ever walked in the mountains. The trail climbs through a time period of more than 100 years of mining and exploration in the Monte Cristo area. Prospectors first explored Silver Creek in the 1870s, but by 1874 mining activity began to die out. Mining had many ups and downs in the Monte Cristo and Silver Creek area. In 1890 a pack trail was built from Scotts Camp (near the starting point of this hike) to 76 Gulch north of Silver Creek. This trail and the Monte Cristo strike in 1889 brought more miners into the area. There were rumors of railroads going up Silver Creek, and Scotts Camp was renamed Galena (after a mineral that is the principal ore in lead) upon rumors of a large smelter that was to be built there. Galena was located at the confluence of the North Fork Skykomish River and Silver Creek. Today several of these mines are still privately owned.

Mineral City (established in the late 1800s) consisted of fifteen city blocks, stores, saloons, hotels, houses, and tents. The town was originally named Silver City. A road was built along the west side of the North Fork Skykomish, but the railroad never came to Silver Creek and the road washed out in a storm. Silver Creek grew isolated and the

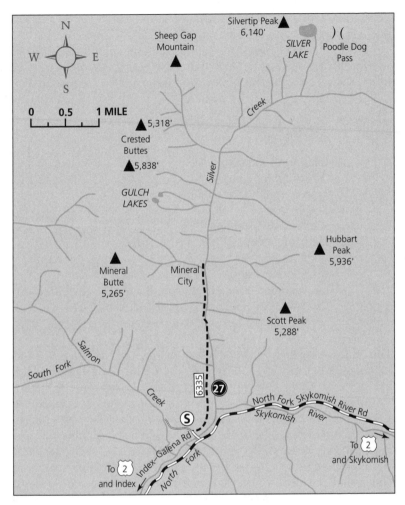

Alaska Gold Rush drew miners away. Today nothing remains of Mineral City, but artifacts can still be found along this historical trail that once climbed all the way to Poodle Dog Pass (4,380 feet) just east of Silver Lake. Occasional reports surface from hikers who have managed to follow the trail all the way to the pass despite having to ford several streams and battle brush. As you hike along this crumbling road, imagine Silver Creek in its heyday with two major settlements, 2,500 mining claims, hundreds of holes in the ground, and trails over high mountain passes to Sultan Basin and Monte Cristo.

The area also interests climbers as well as hikers and history buffs.

There are many peaks for climbers to explore—Silvertip Peak, Mineral Butte, Sheep Gap Mountain, Scott Peak, and Hubbart Peak.

Drive US 2 east past Index and follow the North Fork Skykomish River Road (also called Index–Galena Road or Forest Road 63) about 8.5 miles (past Howard Creek), then turn left to cross the river on a bridge. In 0.2 mile from the bridge, turn right on an unsigned road that is County Road 6335. The hike begins on this road, but there is no official trailhead or facility. The road, one of those "drive until you can't drive any more and that's where the hike starts," is extremely rough and may be driveable for vehicles with high clearance, but it becomes truly impassable at about 1.3 miles and is blocked by boulders and debris. We suggest parking near the beginning of the road. If the road is gated, the hike starts there.

Hike up the road until you come to a road junction; continue straight (right). Shortly past the junction, the road comes to a landslide that may present a challenge to beginning hikers wanting an easy stroll. About 1,000 feet of the road has simply dropped away, but a rough trail (it is rebuilt every year) crosses the rock slide. Experienced hikers can usually cross the landslide without difficulty, and by the peak of the hiking season you'll see a route stomped in by the boots that have gone before you.

The road-trail is very scenic—bring a camera because there is much to photograph, even on a gloomy day. Two mines can be spotted near the beginning of the trail; the Betty Adit is the second mine. The glint of Silver Creek can be seen in a dark gorge dripping with ferns hundreds of feet below and clear green pools where the water pauses between plunging waterfalls. The rocks in the creek and along the road are beautifully colored in mineral tones of gold ocher, burnt sienna, brick red, and orange. There are deep gulches and ravines on both sides of the trail, and the dark vertical walls are slathered with greenery. Every few feet there are waterfalls and several mines along the way. Silvertip Peak and Sheep Gap Mountain are tantalizing glimpses ahead, as is the bright green hanging valley below Poodle Dog Pass.

Loggers left their mark all the way to Silvertip Peak, but where Silver Creek flows through a deep canyon, the forest has been left untouched. The road still has several bridges in place, as far as Mineral City, though much of the road has reverted to trail and it is hard to say how much longer these old bridges can last. Though they were built sturdily and to endure, they are made of wood and the environment is hard on anything people have constructed. Mineral City stood here less than 100 years ago, and it's virtually all gone.

A hiker on the trail to Mineral City

At about 2.5 miles you'll run into an odd sight—an old bus. It belongs to a family who own one of the mines, so respect "NO TRESPASSING" signs and don't leave the road. About 0.5 mile from the town site, a side road descends to Silver Creek.

A short distance from the bus, there is a privately owned cabin off to the left and a hand-painted sign in a nearby tree that reads "DANGER, WOUNDED BEAR." Fortunately we never encountered any wounded bears and we hope you don't either. On the main road-trail, cross the last bridge and at 3 miles reach the site of Mineral City. Most hikers are content to stop at this point because streams crossings beyond here are challenging and bridges are missing.

The trail once continued to Poodle Dog Pass at 4,380 feet, but reports indicate the trail is overgrown and we didn't explore it beyond Mineral City. If you are determined to continue to Poodle Dog Pass, keep in mind that only hikers with cross-country hiking skills and navigation expertise should attempt to reach the pass.

28 TROUBLESOME CREEK

Distance: 0.5-mile loop; 6 miles round trip to wilderness boundary
Difficulty: Moderate
Type of trail: Maintained/abandoned USFS trail
Starting point: 1,200 feet
High point: 1,300 feet, loop; 1,800 feet, wilderness boundary
Elevation gain: 100 feet on loop; 600 feet to wilderness boundary
Hikable: Spring, summer, fall
Map: Green Trails No. 143 Monte Cristo
Information: Skykomish Ranger District, 360-677-2414
Cautions: Brush, routefinding beyond end of nature trail

This old historical trail used by miners may have served as an alternate route into Monte Cristo via Twin Lakes. James Lillis was the first person to prospect and explore Troublesome Creek, in 1874. Lillis Peak (5,319 feet), a technical climb beyond the scope of hikers, is named for him. He discovered the Daisy Mines that are situated on Hubbart Peak. The mines produced gold, silver, and lead. Hubbart Peak (5,936 feet) is the high point of the divide between Troublesome and Silver Creeks, 2.5

miles north of the North Fork Skykomish River. At one time there were mines at all branches of Troublesome Creek and also near the summit of Hubbart Peak. From Hubbart Peak, Joseph Pearsall first saw the rich veins of ore and was inspired to name the place Monte Cristo after the wealthy main character of Alexandre Dumas' novel *The Count of Monte Cristo*. There were other mines in the Troublesome Creek Mining District, such as the Good Luck prospect near the Troublesome Creek Campground. Though the mine is not far from the North Fork Skykomish River Road, the area is full of cliffs and can be hazardous. Another mine, the Shamrock prospect, is located farther downstream between Troublesome Creek and Silver Creek. Warning: Some of these mines may be on private property. Do not trespass and do not enter any mines you encounter.

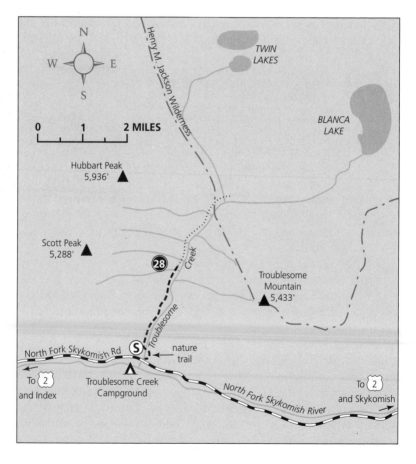

Troublesome Mountain (5,433 feet) takes its name from Troublesome Creek. It was so named by a Northern Pacific engineering party who had a lot of trouble attempting to locate a railroad grade in the area. Hikers enjoy its scenery and history. The trail has been brushed out and can be followed for about 2 miles at present.

Drive US 2 east and turn off at Index. Bypass Index on the North Fork Skykomish River Road (Forest Road 63) and drive 11 miles to the first entrance of the Troublesome Creek Campground (closed in winter). Parking is limited here, but is allowed on the road near the trailhead.

The trail begins in Troublesome Creek Campground as a nature trail that makes a 0.5-mile loop with only 100 feet elevation gain. This easy hike through a fine example of old-growth forest is the most scenic part of the hike. The nature trail loop has two bridges; the lower bridge was closed in 2000 because it had become haz-

Hikers in old-growth forest near Troublesome Creek

ardous, but it has been repaired and the trail is open. Follow the nature trail as it passes under the highway and along the west side of the river. Beginning hikers should not go beyond the nature loop. Hikers and scramblers with cross-country hiking skills and navigational expertise can explore the old trail beyond the nature loop as far as time, energy, skills, and conditions allow.

Look for an unsigned trail just before the bridge; several side paths from the nature loop converge into the old trail. The old trail is pleasant and easy to follow for the first couple of miles. Large trees that have fallen across the old trail have been notched and a stretch of old puncheon remains. The cut logs have been there quite a while and their ends are covered with moss. Compelling Troublesome Creek captures your attention almost as soon as you begin hiking, but equally worthy of attention is the old-growth forest with some of the finest examples of big trees we've seen. Some sections of the trail are brushy where salmonberry and devil's club thrive in this environment. The trail reaches the creek's edge a couple of times, where you can look down on logjams and Troublesome Mountain across the creek. Two fallen trees have become part of the trail—one wonders how long the trees have been there. In June the first mile of trail is especially lovely with carpets of false lily-of-the-valley and ferns.

At about 1.5 miles from the nature trail, you run into flagging; experienced hikers can still find the trail fairly easy to follow a way beyond the flagging—if the flagging is still there. Soon after the flagging, you come across a large fallen cedar tree across the trail and the trail becomes more of a routefinding challenge. Remnants of trail can still be followed beyond the flagging, but the trail soon becomes more elusive. The trail dies at about 2.5 miles past the nature loop (1,800 feet), at about the boundary to the Henry M. Jackson Wilderness. It appears that most hikers have stopped here, a short distance beyond the confluence of two descending creeks, one from Blanca Lake (the main branch of Troublesome Creek), the other from Twin Lakes (the west fork of Troublesome Creek). Beyond the confluence of the creeks the route is cross-country and recommended only for scramblers with mountaineering skills.

29 BECKLER PEAK LOOKOUT SITE

Distance: 6 miles round trip
Difficulty: Extremely challenging
Type of trail: Old road/abandoned trail
Starting point: 3,000 feet
High point: 4,950 feet
Elevation gain: 1,950 feet
Hikable: Spring, summer, fall
Maps: Green Trails No. 175 Skykomish; USGS Skykomish
Information: Skykomish Ranger District, 360-677-2414
Cautions: Brush, difficult cross-country routefinding

Beckler Peak takes its name from E. H. Beckler, chief engineer of the Great Northern Railroad in 1892. The Skykomish River valley was the scene of extensive logging in the 1900s. A lookout tower was estab-

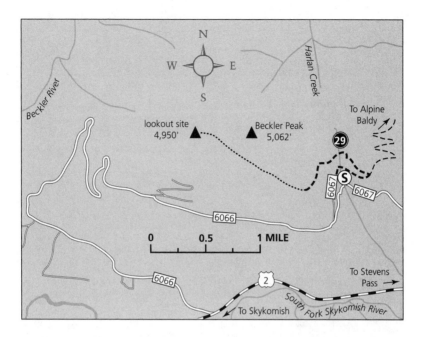

lished by 1924. In 1925 a log cabin was constructed. The route to Beckler Peak originally went straight up the mountain from Skykomish until a horse trail was constructed that switchbacked up the southwest ridge. That trail also accessed Alpine Baldy to the east. In 1935 a 2,700-acre fire swept through the Beckler River area and was fought by men employed by the Civilian Conservation Corps. Though there is no longer evidence of such, a tramway was installed on the last 500 feet of Beckler Peak for hauling supplies and water. In 1950 a winter storm destroyed the lookout tower.

Old maps show trails going to Beckler Peak and Alpine Baldy, but these trails are seldom hiked today. Logging roads have permanently erased most of the old trail, and a clear-cut has added to the confusion. At one time there was talk from the Forest Service of restoring this old trail in the Mount Baker–Snoqualmie National Forest, but a proposal to hook up the trail via Alpine Baldy and Kelley Creek was abandoned when the issue of grizzly bear habitat became insurmountable. As a result, the Beckler Peak/Alpine Baldy area doesn't get many visitors today.

The summit of Beckler Peak (5,062 feet) is not the site of the lookout. The summit, a difficult scramble that falls in that gray area between scrambling and climbing, is not recommended for hikers; however,

sections of the trail can still be hiked today by hikers willing to put up with a bushwhack. Beckler Peak is sometimes done as a winter climb by mountaineers. The lookout site (4,950 feet) on the ridge crest rewards hikers who get that far with views of the Monte Cristo peaks to the north, Mount Daniel to the south, and Skykomish just below. The ridge crest is a dramatic destination with artistic arrangements of boulders, alpine trees, and rock gardens splashed with colorful summer flowers. Lack of publicity about the trails and the ever-present advance of slide alder and brush make this an extremely difficult hike. This exploration is best suited for scramblers with cross-country hiking skills who enjoy exploring historical routes.

Take US 2 east to Forest Road 6066, 2 miles past the Skykomish Ranger Station, and turn left onto it. Road 6066 is in good condition and suitable for passenger cars. Drive the road, staying right at all junctions, until a road junction at 6.5 miles; turn left (uphill) onto Forest Road 6067 (this road is not shown on the 1999 Mount Baker–Snoqualmie National Forest map). Drive a rough 0.5 mile to where the road has been decommissioned and bermed, making it impossible for vehicles to continue.

The hike begins from the berm. As you hike up the road, Tonga Ridge comes into view to the southeast. The first 0.3 mile is a pleasant walk and the brush is manageable. At about 0.3 mile, an unsigned road to the right continues several miles to Alpine Baldy (conditions of the Alpine Baldy trail are unknown). Continue left/straight on Road 6067 as it makes a sweeping switchback, at which point the road deteriorates. The decommissioned road and the brush have made this stretch unpleasant for hikers. It is slow going as the road crosses several small streams, some of which may dry up later in the year.

As you continue on the road, a clear-cut comes into view. Cross a stream at about 0.6 mile (3,400 feet). A short distance from the stream, climb up the dirt bank from the road and climb through the clear-cut, keeping the old-growth forest in sight. Continue climbing through the clear-cut and old-growth forest and find a very faint path heading westerly toward Beckler Peak. Gradually climb about 1,200 feet through brush, using game trails when possible. The ascent is easier if you keep near the edge of the forest. If you reach the ridge crest, you've gone too high and will be cliffed out. Descend a couple hundred feet and look again. If you can't find the old trail, contour a couple hundred feet below the ridge and continue in a westerly direction. The trail is almost

Near the Beckler Peak lookout site

gone, but hikers with routefinding skills may be able to follow the trail to the boulder field below the lookout site at 4,950 feet. A stopping point may not be obvious—stop where it suits you. The views are excellent from the boulder field.

30 KELLEY CREEK TRAIL

Distance: Approximately 6.6 miles round trip
Difficulty: Challenging
Type of trail: Old road/abandoned trail
Starting point: 3,000 feet
High point: 5,000 feet
Elevation gain: 2,000 feet
Hikable: Summer, fall
Maps: Green Trails No. 144 Benchmark Mountain, No. 176
    Stevens Pass; USGS Captain Point, Scenic
Information: Skykomish Ranger District, 360-677-2414
Cautions: Brush, blowdowns, routefinding

This abandoned trail was once part of an extensive 50-mile trail system running east of the Beckler River to the Cascade crest. Much of this trail system has been lost as a result of logging and the proliferation of typical Northwest brush and alder. As trails become more difficult to hike, they are eventually dropped from hiking guides and people stop using them. Information about the Kelley Creek Trail is hard to come by. It is briefly described in the 1988 edition of *100 Hikes in the Glacier Peak Area* (The Mountaineers Books). The trail once went all the way to Scorpion Mountain. In the future the Forest Service hopes to link up this trail with the Iron Goat Trail to the east. Today some sections of the Kelley Creek Trail to Johnson Ridge, located in Mount Baker–Snoqualmie National Forest, can still be hiked, though hikers may have to contend with brush the first mile or so. Hikers willing to bushwhack enjoy this link to Johnson Ridge and Scorpion Mountain.

Drive US 2 east of Skykomish to milepost 55 and turn left on Forest Road 67 (Old Cascade Highway/Road) near Alpine Falls. This is the western end of Road 67—the eastern end rejoins US 2 near Scenic. At 2.2 miles, reach a road junction at Martin Creek Road (Forest Road 6710), and turn left. At about 5.5 miles from US 2, turn left again, onto Spur Road 230. Drive a couple hundred yards, cross a bridge, and park where an overgrown road goes off to the left. There is room for only one or two

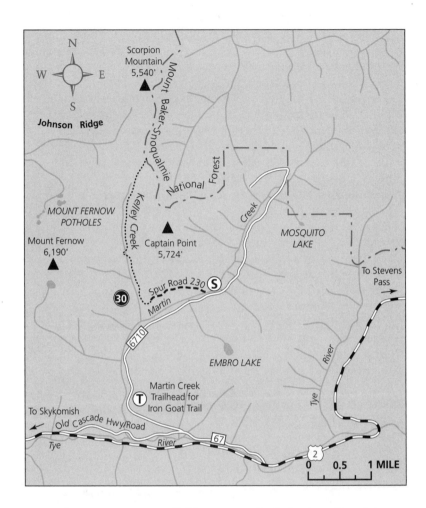

cars, so keep your party small. There are no facilities or trailhead signs.

The overgrown road to the left is the start of the hike. Though the road is rapidly closing in with alders and fireweed, a path can still be followed. A recent report indicates that the road recently has been lopped, making travel easier. In late summer the old road is pretty, with views toward distant peaks framed by stands of fireweed.

There is no clear distinction where the road actually ends and a trail begins. At about 1 mile you may come to a homemade wooden sign on a tree on your left that simply says "TRAIL." By this point you will know you are on a trail of sorts. In about 0.25 mile, find another sign nailed to a tree. The sign reads "JOHNSON RIDGE" and the trail continues to the left. Once you reach this sign, the trail becomes easier to follow. The trail climbs above Kelley Creek for a way, then follows the creek upstream.

At about 1.7 miles (3,600 feet) you come to a major blowdown and a very large tree lying across the trail. This is a confusing area; it is a challenge to find the trail beyond the blowdown. Bear right and you should be able to find it again. The trail makes several switchbacks as it climbs from here, though there are a couple of places where the trail is very faint. Other sections of the trail are surprisingly easy to follow.

The trail crosses a creek with very steep banks; this could be a difficult crossing early in the season. The trail continues on the other side of the creek and is easy to follow to a little under 3 miles (4,500 feet). We stopped here because we were stung several times by yellow jackets, but we could see the trail continuing on. If you lose the trail at this point, you can continue uphill through open forest until you reach the ridge crest. If you are able to follow the trail, you'll come to a junction (there may be a sign) in a meadow at about 3.3 miles (5,000 feet), north of Captain Point at the boundary of Mount Baker–Snoqualmie National Forest.

If you want to keep going, you can turn left and follow the old trail system to Scorpion Mountain (5,540 feet), or turn right to meet the North Crest Cutoff Trail northeast of Captain Point (Hike 31), sometimes referred to as the Johnson Ridge Trail.

31   NORTH CREST CUTOFF TRAIL

Distance: 6.6 miles round trip
Difficulty: Challenging
Type of trail: Logging road/abandoned trail
Starting point: Approximately 3,240 feet
High point: Approximately 5,280 feet
Elevation gain: Approximately 2,040 feet
Hikable: Summer, fall
Maps: Green Trails No. 144 Benchmark Mountain; USGS
   Captain Point
Information: Skykomish Ranger District, 360-677-2414
Cautions: Brush, routefinding

North Crest Cutoff Trail is part of Johnson Ridge Trail No. 1067 and Joan Lake Trail No. 1067.1 in Mount Baker–Snoqualmie National Forest, but it has not been maintained in years. This remnant is part of an old trail system that was still intact through the 1950s, with more than 50 miles of trail. The network of trails radiated from Beckler River east to the Cascade crest and included Evergreen Mountain, Beckler Peak, Alpine Baldy, Scorpion Mountain, Captain Point, and Valhalla Mountain to the Pacific Crest Trail, as well as the Kelley Creek Trail (Hike 30). The trails were built in the 1920s and 1930s for administrative access from the Beckler River Logging Railroad. Road building over the years has shortened this trail system, a major reason the Forest Service abandoned trails in this area except for the section of the Johnson Ridge Trail to Scorpion Mountain and Joan Lake. By 1988 there were only about 20 miles left of the trail system. The North Crest Cutoff Trail is mentioned in the 1988 edition of *100 Hikes in the Glacier Peak Wilderness* (The Mountaineers Books). When that book was written, you could drive to the ridge top, but even then the trail was overgrown and that book's authors recommended that hikers stick to the ridge

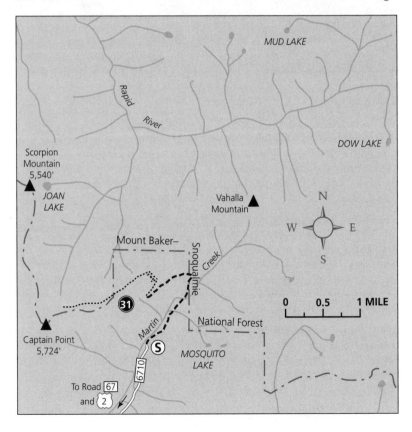

View from the abandoned North Crest Cutoff Trail

crest on a well-traveled trail that crossed two high points.

Only hikers with an avid interest in exploring historical trails find the North Crest Cutoff Trail to be worth the effort. Getting to the trail is not an easy task either because it involves hiking up a logging road to search for an unsigned trailhead, and the trail is difficult to follow. Some sections of the access road are privately owned, though we never encountered "NO TRESPASSING" signs. Hiking the access road could be a problem if logging is ongoing—therefore we advise that you hike logging roads on weekends rather than during the week. Call the Skykomish Ranger District to see if there are any restrictions in the area. In any case, hikers and scramblers with routefinding skills enjoy the solitude of this historical route.

Drive US 2 east a few miles past the Skykomish Ranger Station, and turn left on Forest Road 67 (Old Cascade Highway/Road) near Alpine Falls. This is the western end of Road 67—the eastern end rejoins US 2 near Scenic. Drive 2.2 miles to a road junction at Martin Creek Road (Forest Road 6710), also the access for the Iron Goat Trail, and turn left. Pass the Iron Goat Trailhead (see map for Hike 30) and continue to a junction. Stay right until you come to a gated road (the Martin Creek

Road) at about 5.5 miles from Road 67. Park here and don't block the road because this area is privately owned. If the gate is open, be aware that it can be closed at any time. We recommend that you walk the road even if the gate is open.

From the gate, hike the road past a caretaker's trailer and follow along Martin Creek about 1 mile to a sharp left bend in the road (3,600 feet). Continue climbing as the road goes steeply uphill toward Captain Point. Stay left at all junctions—you climb about 1,200 feet in the next 1.5 miles or so. If you begin to head downhill you've gone the wrong way. At about 2.1 miles (4,800 feet) the way levels out—look for very faint tread through a clear-cut on your left that extends to a patch of old-growth forest. A few ribbons along the route and several cut logs will let you know you're on an old trail.

In a couple hundred feet the trail enters the forest and stays mostly on or near the ridge top. This is old-growth forest at its best and is not brushy. Blowdowns are minor. The trail is fairly easy to follow as long as you stay on the ridge and avoid game trails on either side of the ridge. At about 3.3 miles the trail comes out in the open above a meadow on a high point (about 5,280 feet). This was as far as we explored. The next high point to the west is Captain Point (5,724 feet). From the high point the trail descends 350 feet or so and (according to old maps) contours beneath Captain Point to continue to Scorpion Mountain (5,540 feet). From our high point we could see that the trail appeared to continue.

32 NASON RIDGE

Distance: 6 miles round trip
Difficulty: Challenging
Type of trail: Abandoned
Starting point: Approximately 4,600 feet
High point: Approximately 5,400 feet
Elevation gain: 800 feet
Hikable: Summer, fall
Map: Green Trails No. 144 Benchmark Mountain
Information: Lake Wenatchee Ranger District, 509-763-3103
Cautions: Trail ends abruptly

Nason Ridge is a 18-mile ridge in Okanogan–Wenatchee National Forest that begins near Stevens Pass and heads east. According to A. H. Sylvester, who surveyed and named many lakes and peaks in the Wenatchee district, the ridge was named for a Wenatchee Indian known to whites as Charley Nasen; Mow-mo-nash-et was his Wenatchee name. Nasen had a squatter's claim in the lower valley during early settlement days. Nasen Ridge was named by an unknown source sometime in the late 1800s. Sylvester preferred to keep Native American names. *Na-ta'-poc* was the Native American name for Nason Creek, and Sylvester preserved the Native American name by naming nearby Natapoc Mountain.

Several trails lead to destinations atop Nason Ridge, such as Alpine Lookout, Snowy Creek, Rock Mountain, and Round Mountain. The eastern end of the ridge is now being impacted by logging operations and with the western end of the trail abandoned, most hikers access the middle sections of the trail. It is unfortunate that the section from Rainy Pass to Snowy Creek has dropped out of guidebooks. Most hikers, and even some Forest Service personnel, seem to be unaware of this section of trail. There is talk of trail reconstruction from Rainy Creek to Snowy Creek. At this writing, it is not known whether this reconstruction has been or will be implemented. The first 3 miles of the 4-mile abandoned trail segment are still in fairly good condition. The fourth mile is overgrown and impossible to follow. Experienced hikers with routefinding skills can access views and solitude on this beautiful ridge walk.

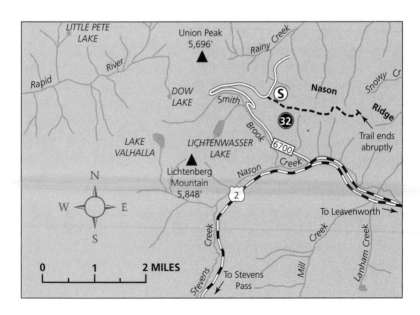

Abandoned section of Nason Ridge

Drive US 2 east of Stevens Pass to Forest Road 6700 (Smith Brook Road) and turn left. Drive about 4 miles to a pond sometimes covered with water lilies at Rainy Pass, where the Smith Brook Road levels off (4,600 feet). The trail can be found on the north side of the pond.

The trail switchbacks through the forest to a high point at about 0.5 mile (5,400 feet), then traverses a meadow beneath another high point on the ridge. Look back for views of the Stevens Pass ski area. The trail descends to 5,200 feet at about 1 mile, stays fairly level for 0.5 mile, then at about 1.5 miles turns left to head north to a saddle on the north side of the ridge. There are views to other drainages and across to clear-cuts. With ups and downs, staying at or near the 5,200-foot level, the trail continues to another saddle at about 2.5 miles as it traverses beneath a high, rocky point (on the north side of the ridge). We hit a snow patch beneath the high point and made the mistake of dropping down from the ridge and losing the trail. We had to retrace our route.

The trail continues to traverse beneath the rocky peak and follows along the ridgeline with views of Glacier Peak and the Monte Cristo peaks before it descends to a boulder field. From the boulder field the trail continues through forest and shrubs before climbing to a saddle at about 3 miles on a north–south ridge, a good viewpoint, and the end of anything resembling a trail. Hikers should stop here and turn around for 6 miles round trip.

Mount Stuart from Ingalls Lake

INTERSTATE 90 WEST OF SNOQUALMIE PASS

33 CCC TRUCK ROAD

> **Distance:** 6.5-mile loop from eastern trailhead to Big
>   Blowout Creek and back; 10 miles one way from
>   eastern trailhead to western trailhead
> **Difficulty:** Moderate
> **Type of trail:** Old road
> **Starting point:** 960 feet
> **High point:** 1,520 feet
> **Elevation gain:** 560 feet
> **Hikable:** Year-round
> **Maps:** Green Trails No. 206 Bandera Mountain; USGS
>   Mount Si
> **Information:** Snoqualmie Ranger District, 425-888-1421
> **Cautions:** Stream crossings

Early in the twentieth century, an old trail climbed out of the Middle Fork Snoqualmie valley to the mines of Dutch Miller Gap. By the 1920s the valley was logged beyond the Taylor River and up the Pratt River Valley. During the Great Depression the Civilian Conservation Corps (CCC), which built trails and roads, bulldozed a rough road up the Middle Fork Snoqualmie valley as far as the old railroad grade near Camp Brown (near the Taylor River). In the 1960s the loggers returned and the Southeast Middle Fork Snoqualmie River Road was built. When the public began to use the new road, the CCC Truck Road was pretty much abandoned except for a short period during the 1980s when logging here in Mount Baker–Snoqualmie National Forest resumed.

Hikers avoided the Middle Fork for years after stories of vandalism and encounters with unsavory characters. Some of the stories were true, but the flavor of the valley has improved. The Forest Service and trail maintenance organizations have put many hours and hard work into making this a safer area to hike. Washington Trails Association, Friends of the Trail, and Volunteers of Washington are just some of the principal players in this ongoing work. Today you are likely to find families camped along the river rather than marathon drinking or shooting parties. Hikers find scenery and solitude that are accessible early in the season. The CCC Truck Road does not get a lot of use from hikers, probably because the road is unsigned and hikers are not aware of it. The road makes a good winter hike that hikers can often enjoy year-round because snow is not generally a problem (the high point of

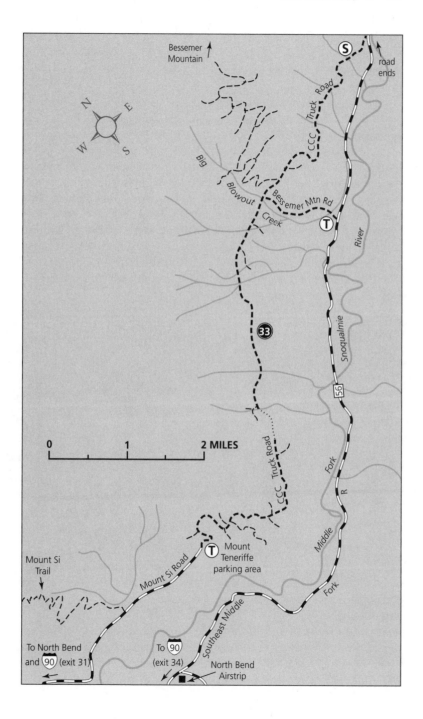

the hike is only 1,520 feet). If the stream crossing at Big Blowout Creek is too challenging, the hike can be shortened by returning to the Southeast Middle Fork Road by way of the Bessemer Mountain Road (about 6 miles round trip).

This hike has two trailheads, and neither is signed. The western trailhead is located at the Mount Teneriffe parking area; the eastern trailhead is located on the Southeast Middle Fork Road. Negotiating the Southeast Middle Fork Road is probably the biggest challenge facing hikers. The 22-mile-long road is subject to potholes, and during winter the upper end usually cannot be driven (or maintained) at all. There is talk of permanently gating the road at Dingford Creek because that section of road is so difficult to maintain. Passenger cars can usually reach the Middle Fork Snoqualmie trailhead and a newly constructed bridge—the Gateway—at 11 miles. For a one-way hike, leave a car at each trailhead and allow time for a car shuttle. Here a loop of part of the CCC Truck Road is described from the eastern trailhead because it is the most scenic segment.

Mountain bikers also enjoy the CCC Truck Road.

Western trailhead: From Interstate 90 take exit 31 into North Bend. From the center of town, go right on Southeast North Bend Way 0.8 mile, then left on Mount Si Road 0.3 mile, across the Middle Fork Bridge. Turn right and drive 3.1 miles to the Mount Teneriffe parking area, 1.1 miles past the Mount Si Trailhead. (The unsigned Mount Si Trailhead is located near the school bus turnaround.) Parking is limited.

Eastern trailhead: From Interstate 90 take exit 34, turn left under the freeway, pass Seattle East Auto Truck Plaza, turn right onto Southeast Middle Fork Snoqualmie River Road 56, and drive 10 miles to the unsigned trailhead. The CCC Truck Road can be seen climbing to the left just before a rock outcropping above the river. Park here; there is room for about four cars, and also parking alongside the road. The Bessemer Mountain Road also is used sometimes as an approach to the CCC Truck Road; it's 7.1 miles from the beginning of the Southeast Middle Fork Snoqualmie River Road.

From the eastern trailhead, hike the CCC Truck Road 0.3 mile to an unmarked road junction and turn left. Beyond the junction, the CCC Truck Road becomes more trail-like as the forest encroaches upon the roadbed. Big leaf maples covered with mosses and lichens create a rainforest ambience. The forest becomes second growth as the road climbs; there are stumps marked with springboard notches. The road comes to a high point with mossy cliffs and views through the trees down to the river, the Pratt River valley, and the Russian Buttes. At about 1.75 miles the road reaches the highest point, about 0.5 mile from the mossy cliffs. The Bessemer Mountain Road can seen climbing on the right as you descend; at about 2.75 miles you reach the junction with it on the right; continue straight.

The CCC Truck Road continues a gentle descent to an unmarked junction with a cairn and Big Blowout Creek at about 3.1 miles (1,280 feet). If crossing the stream is too much of a challenge, take the Bessemer Mountain Road heading down on your left and descend a long mile to the Southeast Middle Fork Road at about 4.25 miles. Turn left on the Southeast Middle Fork Road and walk 2.3 miles back to the eastern trailhead for a 6.5-mile loop.

If you choose to continue south beyond Big Blowout Creek to the western trailhead (instead of returning to the eastern trailhead), you will find that the route becomes less interesting. Clearcuts come into view, and the best of the scenery is left behind. However, you will also find that the old clearcuts and old logging landings provide good places to sit and view the foothills. Avoid side roads and continue on the main road. Near the end of the hike you may find the crumpled remains of a car clinging to a hillside, tangled in the brush. As of 2000 there were no signs indicating the western trailhead. From the end of the road, you will hike past a few private homes (some with barking dogs) before you come to the Mount Teneriffe parking area.

34 RAINY LAKE

Distance: 7 miles round trip
Difficulty: Challenging
Type of trail: Abandoned USFS trail
Starting point: 1,050 feet
High point: 3,764 feet
Elevation gain: Approximately 2,700 feet
Hikable: Spring, summer, fall
Maps: Green Trails No. 174 Mount Si; USGS Lake Philippa
Information: Snoqualmie Ranger District, 425-888-1421
Cautions: Rough primitive trail, difficult routefinding

The Forest Service keeps a low profile on this trail in Mount Baker–Snoqualmie National Forest, mostly because the lake is in the Alpine Lakes Wilderness but also because the trail is rough. Rainy Lake is one of the most special places we've ever been to. You will have to work hard to get there, but it is worth it. Gigantic boulders and old-growth trees frame the lake, creating a garden for giants. One of the more interesting historical aspects of the trail is a bronze plaque on a boulder, honoring George Lewis, a trailblazer who stocked this lake with fish. Rainy Lake was one of his favorite lakes.

Some hikers (including us) discovered this old trail by accident while looking for the Pratt River Trail. In 1999 we hiked downstream from the Gateway Bridge to follow what old-timers called the Ranger Trail (a network of trails that led to backcountry guard stations) to Rainy Creek. We lost the trail several times in brush but got to Rainy Creek, approximately 0.5 mile from the bridge. At Rainy Creek the trail ended in a tangle of brush, but we crossed Rainy Creek on a log and found a trail climbing along the creek. The trail was in good shape—we had found the Rainy Creek Trail. We did not get to the lake, but made plans to return.

Even experienced hikers can easily get lost here. The trail is not mentioned in mainstream hiking guides other than Carl Dreisbach's *Middle Fork Guide* (Big Raven Book, 1997). Dreisbach writes that the

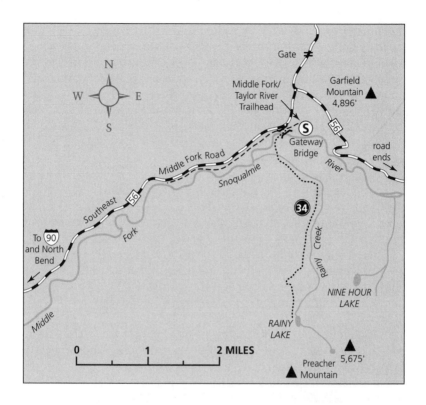

trail exists more in imagination than reality, and the trail challenges even experienced hikers. Sections of the trail are very obscure, but strong hikers with routefinding skills should be able to follow it because much of the trail is fairly straightforward. The flagging we followed in 1999 has been taken down except for one crucial flag that has been left in place to sort out confusion at a very vague junction. Steep sections alternate with level terraces and there are enough glimpses of Garfield Mountain to keep you motivated as the grade steepens. Strong hikers with scrambling and routefinding ability enjoy the lake, waterfalls, old-growth forest, and fishing.

Drive Interstate 90 east to exit 34 and turn left. Pass a cluster of convenience stores and Seattle East Restaurant, and in 0.6 mile turn right onto Southeast Middle Fork Snoqualmie River Road 56; continue 11.6 miles to the Middle Fork Trailhead and Gateway Bridge. Restrooms and water are available.

Cross the Gateway Bridge and turn right on a trail that parallels the Middle Fork. Volunteers have cleared brush from this section of trail, making it much easier to follow. In less than 0.5 mile, look for an unsigned trail heading left (the start of the Rainy Creek Trail). The trail continues a short distance to Rainy Creek. Cross the creek (the log is gone) and climb along the west side of the creek through second-growth forest interspersed with old-growth trees. This is a cool and quiet place on a hot day, and there are no difficulties here. You may notice rolls of old wire along the first section of the trail, once used for storing water in barrels. The lower elevations are lavish with big leaf maple, vine maple, alder, assorted shrubs, moss, lichens, and liverworts (a primitive lichen).

The trail climbs to a talus field and enters the forest again before crossing a second, smaller boulder field. Garfield Mountain comes into view. Sections of the trail now consist of fallen trees, but they are wide enough to walk on (take poles for balance). This is a very pretty section in June with lily-of-the-valley embracing the trunks of old trees. Pockets of deer fern peek from the boulders. Cross several small streams—you may encounter boggy sections near the streams. Up to this point Rainy Creek is on your left as you climb with partial views of waterfalls along the way.

At about 2.5 miles the trail begins to veer away from Rainy Creek and stays mostly in deep forest. Here you cannot see landmarks, and this is where you might have to work a little harder to stay on the trail. Follow the trail, such as it is, through brush and over logs until you hear the sounds of another creek. The trail follows this creek for a short distance and comes to a crossing at about 3 miles (3,160 feet). We hope that no one has taken down the crucial flag that marks this spot. If the flag is gone, look carefully for a faint trail leading to the creek. After crossing the creek, the faint route heads uphill in an easterly direction. The creek you have crossed is not Rainy Creek, and this is where many hikers have gone astray because they continued to follow the creek rather than cross it (believing it to be Rainy Creek). This is a small creek that doesn't appear on the Green Trails map. From the crossing the trail begins a very steep climb to a ridge above Rainy Lake.

There are more expansive views of Garfield Mountain and soon the cliffs above Rainy Lake come into view. At the ridge crest at about 3 miles, look down to Rainy Lake and find a rough path that descends to the outlet stream and lakeshore. Follow the path around the lake on the right-hand side to an area where there are a couple of primitive

Crossing Rainy Creek

campsites at 3.5 miles. The sharp peak above the lake is Point 5675. The lake is far enough for most hikers.

Very strong hikers and fishermen have hiked cross-country to Nine Hour Lake from Rainy Lake, but it is a hazardous cross-country route that is not recommended.

35　MARTEN LAKE

Distance: 8 miles round trip
Difficulty: Challenging
Type of trail: Road/way trail
Starting point: 1,200 feet
High point: Approximately 2,950 feet
Elevation gain: 1,750 feet
Hikable: Spring, summer, fall
Maps: Green Trails No. 174 Mount Si; USGS Lake Philippa,
　　Snoqualmie Lake
Information: Snoqualmie Ranger District, 425-888-1421
Cautions: Brush, rough terrain, avalanche danger early in
　　season, difficult routefinding

Beautiful Marten Lake is reached via the Taylor River Road, which is no longer open to vehicles. At the turn of the twentieth century, the only trail in the Middle Fork Snoqualmie River valley was an access trail to the Dutch Miller mines. By the 1920s railroad logging in Mount Baker–Snoqualmie National Forest was going strong, and rail lines were constructed beyond the Taylor River. The loggers were followed by the Civilian Conservation Corps (CCC), who constructed a track from the Mount Si road to meet the railroad grade near Camp Brown near the Taylor River. By the end of World War II, the road had become a recreational thoroughfare for cars and jeeps. The loggers returned in the 1960s to cut the old growth that was beyond the reach of the old railroads, and the road built by the CCC was abandoned. The Southeast Middle Fork Road was constructed and was open to the public. By the late 1980s most of the logging was complete.

In summer, sections of the Marten Lake trail become a streambed, so it is advised to save this hike for a dry day. Even though volunteers have cleared brush, the wet vegetation that remains will give you a good soaking. This hike is recommended for hikers who enjoy isolation and are willing to bushwhack to a great destination.

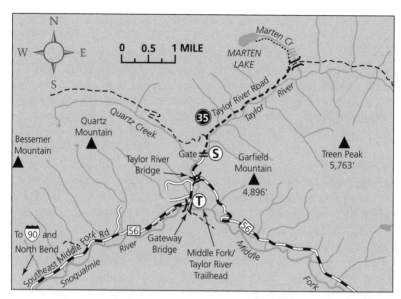

From Interstate 90 take exit 34 to Seattle East (also known as Ken's Truck Town) and turn left. Drive under the freeway, pass convenience stores, turn right on Southeast Middle Fork Snoqualmie River Road 56, and drive 12 miles to the Taylor River Bridge. Just beyond is a Y intersection. Go left (straight) 0.5 mile on rough road to the gated bridge over the Taylor River.

The Marten Lake Trail begins on the gated Taylor River Road, which generally is snowfree by mid- to late April. At 0.4 mile is the junction for the Quartz Creek Road; continue straight. Just past this junction, the Taylor River Road crosses a stream that can be a challenge during heavy rain or snowmelt. The road-trail parallels the Taylor River, with tempting side trails and camps along the way. In mid-April flowers line the road—trilliums, coltsfoot, violets, salmonberry, flowering currant, and false lily-of-the-valley carpet the ground. Later in the season you'll see bleeding heart, columbine, and rosy twisted stalk. The dramatic peak that dominates the sky is Garfield Mountain (4,896 feet).

Continue climbing; at just under 3 miles, begin looking for an unsigned trail going off on the left—it is directly across from a huge cedar snag. If you get to Marten Creek Falls and the bridge, you've missed it. Walk back down the road until you spot it. The adventure begins as soon as you leave the Taylor River Road—this route is not recommended for beginning hikers.

Cross a large fallen log any way you can and follow faint tread through old-growth forest along the south side of Marten Creek, sometimes within sight of the creek and always within earshot of it. The trail is wet and muddy in sections, even on a dry day. Volunteers have cleared out much of the brush along the trail, but it is still challenging. There are also wet, slippery rocks and roots to contend with. Keep going; it's worth it. The trail wanders through impressive sections of old growth the loggers didn't take. Ancient cedars stand silently beside the trail, some of them 12 feet in diameter.

The route is vague in spots—if you reach a dead end, try again. When faced with multiple paths, take the one that looks the most well-traveled. Soon boxcar-size boulders loom over the trail, and more boulders can be seen through the trees. One large boulder has a stand of small trees growing on its top. The trail, such as it is, goes underneath and around the boulders to an open area and crosses a boulder field that is prone to avalanche early in the season. In summer the slope is a green blaze of alder, vine maple, salmonberry, and huckleberry. In mid-April most of this open area is still under snow and undercut by several channels of water making their way to Marten

Marten Lake

Creek. If there is snow, tread carefully and probe with a pole before stepping across. Snow melts out from underneath—take care that you don't fall through.

The way trail becomes a steep scramble path of rocks and roots. Shortly before reaching the lake at 4 miles, the trail levels off and in June marsh marigolds can be seen. There is a large campsite at the outlet stream of the lake, which has flat slabs of rock that form a series of waterfalls that can be glimpsed from the trail. Occasional hikers and fishermen frequent this lake. This is a very pristine area—if you visit, keep your party small.

36 SNOW LAKE VIA ROCK CREEK

Distance: 11.6 miles round trip
Difficulty: Challenging
Type of trail: Maintained USFS trail
Starting point: 1,500 feet
High point: 4,100 feet
Elevation gain: 2,600 feet
Hikable: Spring, summer, fall
Maps: Green Trails No. 207 Snoqualmie Pass, No. 175 Skykomish
Information: Snoqualmie Ranger District, 425-888-1421
Cautions: Rough access road, brush

Snow Lake, in the Alpine Lakes Wilderness, is one of the most popular hikes in the state of Washington. The trailhead is close to Seattle, the elevation gain is not great, it is absolutely gorgeous, and the trail is maintained and easy to access. For those reasons, the trail is crowded and often serves as the poster child for the trail that has been loved to death. Who doesn't love Snow Lake? Some hikers have stopped going to Snow Lake because it is too popular. Maybe they haven't heard of the Rock Creek approach to the lake, even though it is featured in hiking guides. This alternate route can be accessed from Dingford Creek via the Middle Fork Snoqualmie River Trail. It is a much quieter way to reach the lake, and on a weekend day in midsummer you may be the only hiker on the path.

The trails in the Middle Fork Snoqualmie River valley provide access to an area rich in history. The river valley was used by miners,

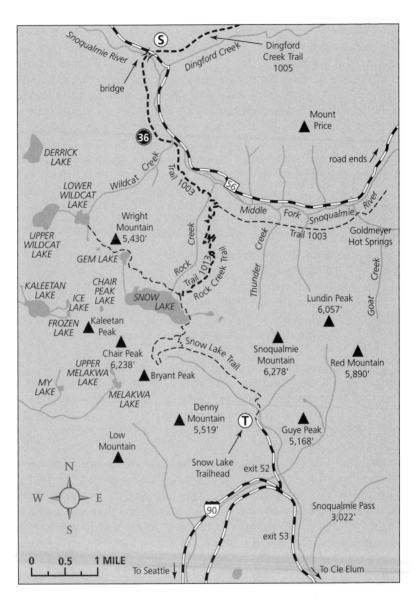

trappers, loggers, hunters, and homesteaders long ago, and their traces remain. The area was logged extensively in the 1920s and '30s, with logging continuing from time to time on private timber-company land. Many pockets of old-growth forest can still be found.

The valley had an unsavory reputation for many years in the latter part of the twentieth century as the Middle Fork Snoqualmie River Road became a favorite hangout for thrill seekers and beer drinkers. Many hikers stopped hiking in the area when stories began to appear about vandalized cars at trailheads and other crimes. Fortunately the nature of the river valley has changed, thanks to the efforts of volunteers such as Friends of the Trail, Washington Trails Association, and Volunteers for Washington. Since the Forest Service has suffered severe budget cuts, many of the trails in the area would not survive without the hours of work put in by these volunteers. Work parties have removed abandoned cars and cleaned up garbage strewn in campsites along the river. Families have begun to return, and as more hikers visit the area, the unsavory characters who used to frequent the area have moved on.

Another reason this route may be used less frequently by hikers is the access road. Hikers must face the challenge of the infamous Southeast Middle Fork Snoqualmie River Road (Forest Road 56), which is usually in bad condition and never in good condition. The hike begins from the Dingford Creek Trailhead, 6 rough miles beyond the Taylor River Bridge, for a total of 18 bone-jarring miles of driving.

Some of these trails can be hiked at least in part throughout the year, depending on conditions. The snowline is usually around 3,000 feet near Garfield Mountain, and lower up the valley. Hikers often don't run into significant snow in winter until the Taylor River Bridge at 12 miles, but it varies from season to season. Hikers can sometimes drive to the new Middle Fork/Taylor River Trailhead (see map for Hike 35) on New Year's Day without a trace of snow. In 1998 the Rock Creek Trail was in reasonable condition, with the exception of 0.5 mile of brush near the end of the trail. Hikers with trailfinding skills enjoy this lonesome approach to one of the most scenic lakes in the region. Experienced hikers can make a one-way 9.8-mile hike by leaving a car at the Snow Lake Trailhead (at the end of the Alpental road off Interstate 90 at exit 52), using a car shuttle.

From Interstate 90 take exit 34, turn left under the freeway, pass Seattle East (Ken's Truck Town), and turn right on Road 56 (Southeast Middle Fork Snoqualmie River Road). Drive 12 miles to the Taylor River Bridge and turn right to continue 6 miles to Dingford Creek Trail No. 1005.

Hike down to the Snoqualmie River on the trail and cross the Middle Fork on a bridge. Turn left onto the Middle Fork Snoqualmie River Trail No. 1003. This is a very pretty stretch of trail as the route

passes clear, green pools and sections of old growth before leaving the river and coming to a crossing of Rock Creek at 1.25 miles. After the creek crossing, the trail climbs to parallel Rock Creek before leveling off to follow an old railroad grade. About 0.25 mile past the crossing, the trail comes to the junction for the Rock Creek Trail, the midway point between Dingford Creek and Goldmeyer Hot Springs (1,630 feet).

Head south on the Rock Creek Trail (Trail No. 1013), which soon begins a steep climb. The trail is in surprisingly good condition as it climbs through second-growth forest strewn with large boulders carpeted with years of moss. There are sections of old growth where it looks as if the moss hasn't been disturbed in decades. Hikers find many places to stop and rest on a warm day before the trail breaks out into the open. At 2.75 miles there are views of Garfield Mountain to the northeast, and at 3.75 miles you have views through the trees to a waterfall and the Rock Creek headwall.

At 5.25 miles there's a 0.5-mile stretch of brush and loose rocks, the most challenging part of the route. Once you have worked your way through the brush (sometimes routefinding with your feet rather than your eyes), the trail climbs up and over a rocky rib to meet the Snow Lake Trail at 5.8 miles. Walk in either direction to explore the lakeshore.

37 CASCADE CREST TRAIL TO RED PASS (OLD PACIFIC CREST TRAIL)

Distance: 5.6 miles round trip to Red Pass
Difficulty: Challenging
Type of trail: Abandoned USFS trail
Starting point: 3,000 feet
High point: 5,350 feet
Elevation gain: 2,350 feet
Hikable: Summer, fall
Maps: Green Trails No. 207 Snoqualmie Pass; USGS
   Snoqualmie Pass (1961) 15-minute, Snoqualmie Pass
   (1989) 7.5-minute
Information: Snoqualmie Ranger District, 425-888-1421
Cautions: Brush, stream crossings, routefinding

Hikers sometimes refer to the abandoned Cascade Crest Trail as the Old Commonwealth Basin Trail or Old Pacific Crest Trail. Years ago the

Popular Snow Lake has more than one approach.

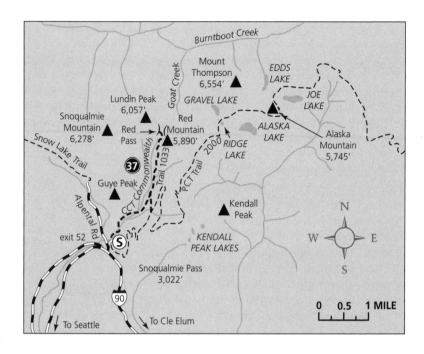

PCT climbed to Red Pass before descending the Goat Creek valley to the Middle Fork Snoqualmie River Trail No. 1003. In the 1970s the Old PCT had two routes. A pack route went up the trail toward Snow Lake, climbed above Source Lake, then dropped down to Snow Lake before descending to the Middle Fork Snoqualmie via Rock Creek. The hikers route went up Commonwealth Basin and over Red Pass, then descended Goat Creek to Goldmeyer Hot Springs. The route down from Red Pass often involved a steep descent on hard, icy snow. The trail lived up to its reputation as being a "tough" trail.

Today the CCT can still be followed quite easily to Red Pass because many hikers who know about the trail continue to use it. This abandoned trail is in better condition than many other abandoned trails. Beyond Red Pass the trail becomes more challenging because the section between Red Pass and the Middle Fork Snoqualmie have become overgrown. From Red Pass the trail descends and follows a ridge west of Goat Creek, staying high above the creek. Volunteers have cleared some of the brush between Red Pass and the Middle Fork Snoqualmie, and today strong hikers with routefinding ability can follow the old trail once again. Most hikers will want an ice ax or poles (with or without snow) because the terrain is very steep. In 2000 the route was clear to 3,300 feet (about 2,000 feet below Red Pass). The Cascade Crest Trail came out at Burntboot Creek. Backpackers often stopped at Goldmeyer Hot Springs, a privately owned enterprise that requires advance reservations. Red Pass is far enough for most hikers and makes a splendid destination with dramatic views of Mount Rainier and the Snoqualmie Pass peaks. Hikers with trailfinding skills enjoy the area's solitude, history, and scenery.

Drive Interstate 90 to Snoqualmie Pass and take exit 52. Turn left on Alpental Road, drive a short distance, and follow the signs for the Pacific Crest Trail No. 2000 parking lot.

The Cascade Crest Trail (Trail No. 1033) starts from the Pacific Crest Trailhead at Snoqualmie Pass. A short distance from the parking lot, look

View from the Cascade Crest Trail
Photo by Steve Fox

An old PCT blaze found on the Cascade Crest Trail
Photo courtesy of Steve Fox

for an unsigned trail going off to the left. Follow this trail toward Commonwealth Basin, at unmarked junctions turning right. In September 2000 the CCT was in good condition with only a few minor blowdowns. The trail stays fairly level until it crosses Commonwealth Creek at about 0.3 mile. Hikers find many places to camp along Commonwealth Creek. This makes a good beginner's backpacking trip, though Commonwealth Basin is easier to access from the Pacific Crest Trail.

As the old trail climbs beside Commonwealth Creek, hikers may encounter some confusion where the trail crosses the creek. If you lose the trail at the creek, look around for it and if you can't find it, go back the way you came and follow the Pacific Crest Trail to Commonwealth Basin. Beyond the last stream crossings at about 0.8 mile, the rest of the CCT route to Red Pass is easy to follow.

From the creek the trail climbs steeply toward Red Pass in a series of switchbacks. Once you leave the basin, more of the route is open, with occasional pockets of forest. At about 1.3 miles a spur trail from the PCT comes in from the right. Look for an "ABANDONED TRAIL" sign near the junction. Stay left on the CCT. The Cascade Crest Trail climbs and contours beneath Red Mountain. A small lake can be seen from the trail.

Red Mountain can be scrambled from the trail, but the rock is loose and the climb is recommended only for experienced scramblers. The steep basin is prone to avalanche in winter and spring—only experienced climbers with ice axes and snowshoes should consider it.

The trail climbs to the ridge crest that overlooks the valley below and surrounding peaks. Mount Thompson comes into view as the trail follows the ridgeline toward Red Pass. At 2.8 miles reach Red Pass; look for a tree with an old Pacific Crest Trail sign that was spotted as recently as September 2000. There are views everywhere you look— Guye Peak, Red Mountain, Kendall Peak, Thompson, Snoqualmie Mountain, Lundin Peak—but Mount Rainier takes center stage on a clear day.

Hikers can follow an easy way trail from Red Pass that climbs 350 feet to a high point with more views. This trail goes nearly to the summit of Lundin; hikers should stop here because climbing skills and equipment are required beyond this point.

Hikers with cross-country and navigational skills can descend Red Pass to Burntboot Creek (about 2.5 miles from the pass), but should expect brush and routefinding challenges.

Experienced hikers can devise a 5.6-mile loop via the Commonwealth Basin. To do so, start from Pacific Crest Trail No. 2000 at

Snoqualmie Pass, hike north 2.5 miles to the junction for Common-wealth Basin, then continue about 1.1 miles to Red Pass. Return to the PCT trailhead on the CCT in 2.8 miles; in Commonwealth Basin, stay left at unsigned junctions. The Cascade Crest Trail ends at the Pacific Crest Trail a short distance from the parking lot; turn right to the parking lot.

38 SILVER PEAK

Distance: 6 miles round trip
Difficulty: Moderate
Type of trail: Maintained USFS way trail
Starting point: 3,800 feet
High point: 5,605 feet
Elevation gain: 1,805 feet
Hikable: Summer, fall
Maps: Green Trails No. 207 Snoqualmie Pass; USGS
     Snoqualmie Pass (15-minute)
Information: Snoqualmie Ranger District, 425-888-1421
Cautions: None

Silver Peak was a favorite destination of The Mountaineers in the 1930s. Many peaks in the Snoqualmie area were named by The Mountaineers because they made many first ascents. The route is described in the 1931 Mountaineers Annual by H. R. Morgan: "Take the Silver Peak Trail to Olalee Meadows. Here take a trail which branches off on the right about seventy-five yards beyond Olalee Creek and leads to the timbered ridge immediately below and to the north of the peak. From here the route follows the bed of a gully to a cirque at about 5,000 feet elevation, and thence up and over the low ridge flanking the cirque on the west. The rest of the way to the summit keeps just below the crest of the ridge on the west side." The Mountaineers placed a summit register on Silver Peak in 1916, and they also succeeded in reaching the summit on snowshoes in 1918.

Late September or early October is a good time to explore this trail, as fall colors are at their peak. With the sun low in the sky, the views of the Snoqualmie peaks are outstanding on a clear day despite the juxtaposition of clear-cuts and logging roads, all part of the "checkerboard" created by railroad land grants in the nineteenth century. In winter Silver Peak is often done as a snowshoe trip (or a

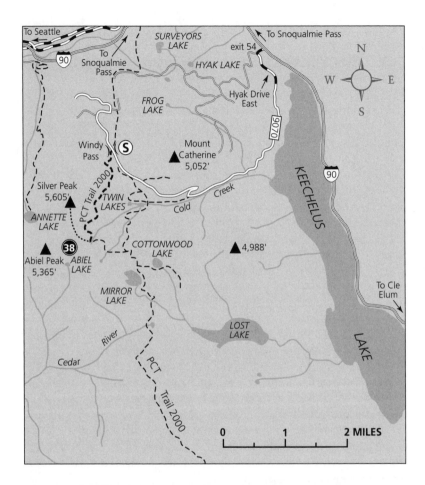

winter scramble) from Annette Lake when avalanche danger is low. Hikers with scrambling skills find other tempting summits in this area—Abiel and Tinkham Peaks are nearby. All three peaks can be climbed in a day by strong climbers. Of the three peaks, Silver Peak is the easiest and is considered a nontechnical "walk-up." The way trail to Silver Peak is not really an abandoned trail, but the cross-country route from Pacific Crest Trail (PCT) No. 2000 in Mount Baker–Snoqualmie National Forest doesn't show on maps nor is it featured in guidebooks. The route is a good example of a way trail, a trail created by scramblers on their way to Silver Peak. Hikers have views of Mounts Rainier, Stuart, and Baker, as well as the Snoqualmie peaks.

From Interstate 90 take exit 54. At an unsigned road junction in

0.3 mile (near the beginning), stay left. Drive through Hyak Estates on Hyak Drive East. Continue on the road and pass a sewage treatment plant. Just past the sewage treatment plant, turn onto Forest Road 9070 and drive 4.6 miles, passing trailheads for Cold Creek, Mount Catherine, and Twin Lakes, to the Pacific Crest Trailhead at Windy Pass. The trailhead is on the left side of the road but is not signed as the PCT. The old, weathered sign can barely be read as "MIRROR LAKE." Oddly, the PCT trail marker is on the other side of the sign. Look for a wide place to park along the road near the trailhead.

Turn left on the PCT as the trail crosses an open meadow with mountain ash and huckleberry, an area referred to as Olallie Meadows in some trail guides. *Olallie* means "berry" in the Chinook language. The area is a paradise for hikers in search of berries. Within 0.25 mile pass a small pond; on a clear day, the Snoqualmie peaks can be seen from here. The PCT is wide and easy to follow; the scenery is superb. It is hard to believe that civilization is close as the trail goes through quiet old-growth forest interspersed with open areas of rock gardens and sparkling tarns. Silver and Tinkham Peaks can be seen from several points along the trail.

At about 0.5 mile, avoid a way trail heading uphill beneath a rocky outcropping. This path may be another route up Silver Peak, but the terrain appears steeper and more of a climbing route than the easier way trail. Continue on the PCT and pass two trail mileage signs reading "5" and "6." Just past the "6" marker, the trail descends in a series of switchbacks. From marker "6" it is about 0.5 mile to where an obvious unsigned trail (the abandoned Gardiner Trail) takes off uphill to the right through the trees at about 1.8 miles from the trailhead. Apparently the Gardiner Trail was closed because a section of it was in the Cedar River watershed.

The trail is easy to spot if you are looking for it. If you miss it and come to an open area with a pond on your left and a meadow on your right, another obvious trail heading uphill also gets you there. The trail in the meadow soon joins the main path (the old Gardiner Trail) that climbs to the ridge crest in about 400 feet. The trail is straightforward and easy to follow. At the crest of the ridge, look for an unsigned trail junction. Turn right for Silver Peak. From the ridge crest the trail climbs 800 feet in a scant mile to the summit of Silver. The last 0.5 mile is in the open, with a long climb up a talus field. So many hikers have gone this way that the path is apparent and can even be seen from below.

Descending Silver Peak

The climb along the ridge is scenic with views of the Snoqualmie peaks, small tarns, and clumps of subalpine trees.

The last 200 feet is an easy scramble and not at all technical unless there is snow. The summit is rocky with several viewpoints and enough room for several hikers. Annette Lake is directly below; to the south is Mount Rainier. On a clear day Mount Stuart can be seen, and even a glimpse of Mount Baker is possible. Closer by are Tinkham and Abiel Peaks, Granite Mountain, and McClellan Butte.

In the Teanaway

INTERSTATE 90 EAST OF SNOQUALMIE PASS

39 LITTLE KACHESS TRAIL

Distance: 9.2 miles round trip
Difficulty: Moderate
Type of trail: Maintained/occasionally maintained
   USFS trail
Starting point: 2,300 feet
High point: 2,550 feet
Elevation gain: 250 feet
Hikable: Spring, summer, fall
Maps: Green Trails No. 207 Snoqualmie Pass, No. 208
   Kachess Lake
Information: Cle Elum Ranger District, 509-674-4411
Cautions: Stream crossing

Little Kachess Trail No. 1312, which is not featured in most hiking guides, appears in some guidebooks as the Lakeshore Trail and in others as the Little Kachess Trail. An old trailhead sign along the path is signed Kachess Lake Trail. Whatever you want to call this trail, it is the lower

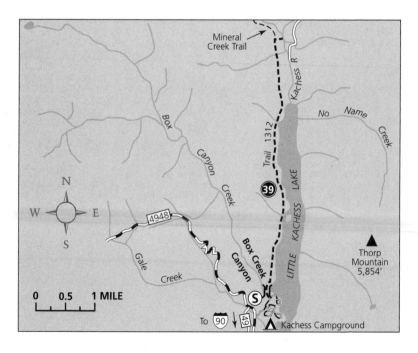

part of an old trail in Okanogan-Wenatchee National Forest that climbs to Mineral Creek Park in the Alpine Lakes Wilderness. The junction for the Mineral Creek Trail, at the north end of Little Kachess Lake, makes a good turnaround point. In May the lower section of the trail is a flower walk.

Drive Interstate 90 east of Snoqualmie Pass and take exit 62. Turn left (northwest) and drive about 6 miles on Forest Road 49 to Kachess Campground, where the trail starts. There are facilities when the campground is open. If it is closed, park at the gate (don't block the gate, because Forest Service personnel may be at work in the campground) and walk in to the trailhead. If trailhead signs are not in place yet, walk or drive into the campground; go to the north end of the campground and a large parking area where the Little Kachess Trail begins. (The upper end of the trail, at the Mineral Creek Trailhead, can also be accessed from the Cooper Pass Road.)

This island in Little Kachess Lake can be seen from the trail.

The first 0.25 mile of the trail is barrier free, with plenty of places to sit and enjoy the scenery. After crossing Box Creek Canyon on a bridge, the trail parallels the lakeshore with several ups and downs. The barrier-free section of trail ends at a closed-in viewpoint above the lake. Find the old trailhead sign ("KACHESS LAKE") near the viewpoint and look for the trail heading uphill. It hadn't been maintained in early May 2000 but the trail was in good condition, and most hikers should be able to hike the trail without difficulty. The next section of the trail is the most scenic, with several mossy boulders providing overlooks to the lake. A waterfall can be seen on the other side of the lake. At about 1.5 miles, look for a view of a small island near the lakeshore.

The next section of trail is a mix of open areas and forest with occasional glimpses of old clear-cuts above the lake. The trail comes to a waterfall and stream crossing—in spring this crossing can be challenging. Then the trail descends to an old mining road that follows along the lake and climbs above it to meet the junction for the Mineral Creek Trail at 4.6 miles. Most hikers stop here.

40 HOWSON CREEK TRAIL

Distance: 7 miles round trip
Difficulty: Challenging
Type of trail: Recently reopened USFS trail
Starting point: 2,300 feet
High point: 5,300 feet
Elevation gain: 3,000 feet
Hikable: Summer, fall
Maps: Green Trails No. 208 Kachess Lake; USGS Cle
  Elum Lake
Information: Cle Elum Ranger District, 509-674-4411
Cautions: Boulder field, vague tread

In May and early June, many hikers begin seeking the high country and probing the snow line on trails in the eastern Cascades because these trails generally melt out earlier. The Teanaway is an extremely popular hiking area, bordered by the Wenatchee Mountains and the Cle Elum River on the west, Teanaway Ridge on the east, and Wenatchee National Forest on the south. The Teanaway is a major river with several forks—other rivers and tributaries are Fortune Creek, Boulder Creek, and the Cle Elum River. The area is dry, the soil thin and rocky. Hemlock, Douglas fir, and grand fir can be found on the west slopes of the Cle Elum valley, but on the east side lodgepole pine, white pine, ponderosa pine, and Douglas fir prevail. The ridge tops are too dry to support much vegetation other than brushy evergreens, buck brush, and a few trees. The Yakama Indians were the first to explore and inhabit the Cle Elum valley. They established several trails in the area. White men entered the district in the 1870s to prospect and mine for minerals. The miners pioneered many of the roads and trails in existence today. Loggers followed the miners. The loggers harvested Douglas fir and ponderosa pine at lower elevations while mining continued in the upper regions. Mining continued until the 1950s, but

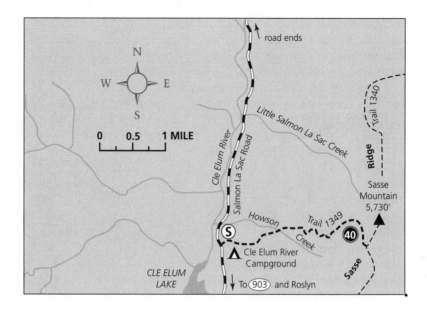

there is little mining activity today. Old roads, prospect holes, and ruins tell many unwritten stories.

Howson Creek Trail No. 1349 is an old trail that has recently been reopened by the Cle Elum Ranger District. The trail can usually be hiked by late June, though there may be some snow patches lingering on the high point, Sasse Ridge. Horses and mountain bikes are allowed on the trail, but motorized vehicles are prohibited. We found the trail easy to follow despite some sections where the tread was vague. The reconstructed trail intersects an old trail and game trails at several points, and confusion is possible. If you get off route, the old trail and the new trail are close enough together that you should be able to get to Sasse Ridge without getting lost. The upper sections of trail are dry except for patchy snow, so later in summer carry plenty of water. This is a very hot trail in midsummer. Hikers with trailfinding skills enjoy the impressive views of Lemah Mountain and Mount Rainier, and the trail is lonesome enough to make it worthwhile. In early June the first couple miles of the trail are abundant with wildflowers—two varieties of Indian paintbrush, penstemon, lupine, luina, and chocolate lilies near the creek.

Drive Interstate 90 east to the Roslyn exit, exit 80. Drive northwest on State Route 903 through the small town of Roslyn. From Roslyn drive northwest on the Salmon La Sac Road for 10.9 miles, 6 miles past the Last Resort. The signed trailhead can be found on the right-hand side of the road. The sign is small and easy to miss. There is room for a few cars near the trailhead, but there are no facilities.

The trail begins as an old jeep track as it climbs to a crossing of Howson Creek at about 1 mile (3,000 feet). At a junction just before the crossing, turn left—a sign indicating "TRAIL" points the way, the only signage along the route. In June the crossing was not a problem. Beyond the creek, the trail climbs steeply through an old clear-cut. On a hot day this section is grueling, but there are shaded sections along the trail. The clear-cut ends at approximately 1.3 miles (about 3,300 feet). Beyond the clear-cut, the trail switchbacks through forest with glimpses of Lemah Mountain and Cle Elum Lake below. As the trail climbs, it begins to deteriorate, with narrow tread and loose rock. There are a few blowdowns to contend with, but none of them present major obstacles.

At about 2 miles (4,000 feet) the trail comes to the edge of a large boulder field, then enters the forest again. There are a couple of blowdowns and a few game trails in this wooded section. Head uphill if you lose the trail, and you should be able to pick it up again. Though the trail is not cairned in the boulder field, we were able to follow it fairly easily. At about 2.5 miles (about 5,000 feet) the trail levels a bit as it contours beneath Sasse Ridge. Mount Rainier comes into view. The trail continues across the boulder field to a saddle at 3.5 miles (5,300 feet)—in June there was snow—but there was no trail sign indicating we had intersected Sasse Ridge. This is where most hikers should stop. The views are good and there isn't a great deal more to be gained by

A hiker enjoys the view from the Howson Creek Trail.

continuing on because the summit of Sasse Mountain is forested.

If your heart is set on a summit climb, walk cross-country a scant 0.5 mile through patchy snow in the trees on a vague trail to the forested summit of Sasse Mountain (5,730 feet), the high point of this long ridge. Experienced hikers with navigational skills can make a loop by hiking down Sasse Mountain Trail No. 1340 either north or south, with many cross-country options for returning to the Salmon La Sac Road.

41 RED MOUNTAIN VIA LITTLE JOE LAKE

Distance: 5 miles round trip
Difficulty: Moderate
Type of trail: Occasionally maintained USFS trail
Starting point: 3,550 feet
High point: 5,707 feet, lookout site
Elevation gain: 2,157 feet
Hikable: Summer, fall
Maps: Green Trails No. 208 Kachess Lake; USGS Polallie Ridge
Information: Cle Elum Ranger District, 509-674-4411
Cautions: Stream crossings

Red Mountains seem to pop up everywhere in Washington, though Red Mountain near Cle Elum Lake is probably the most lonesome. This district was home to several lookouts in earlier times—today only the Thorp Mountain lookout and Red Top on Teanaway Ridge are standing, two of the few remaining lookouts in the Wenatchee National Forest. The Red Mountain lookout site was destroyed in 1948. Not much remains except clumps of melted glass and a few nails. This is a very scenic ridge and the views are awesome: Cle Elum Lake to the south; a hazy Mount Rainier to the southwest; Thorp Mountain to the west; and Davis Peak, Jolly Mountain, and Mount Stuart to the east. A few bleached snags add character to the stony ridge.

Two small lakes, Thorp Lake and Little Joe Lake, are located in the northern section of the district. Little Joe Lake is in the process of evolving into terra firma—the lake is very shallow and the lakeshore is filling in with grasses. Little Joe Lake and Red Mountain are not included in the Alpine Lakes Wilderness. These and other trails in the district such as the No-Name Ridge Trail are in danger of being logged as a result of a recent Plum Creek land exchange. As of this writing, the fate of some of these trails is unknown. Therefore, it is suggested you call the Cle Elum Ranger District for an update on trail and road conditions.

The trail to Little Joe Lake is an old trail. Apparently a trail once climbed all the way from the Salmon La Sac guard station to Red Mountain. The trail to Little Joe Lake is described in the *Cle Elum Ranger District Hiking Guide;* however, the trail from Little Joe Lake to Red Mountain doesn't show on maps. The scramble of Red Mountain is described in the out-of-print *Teanaway Country* by Mary Sutliff (Signpost Publications, 1980). The Cle Elum Ranger District is putting trail fees to good use and reopening old trails such as the Howson Creek Trail (Hike 40) and performing limited maintenance on other trails,

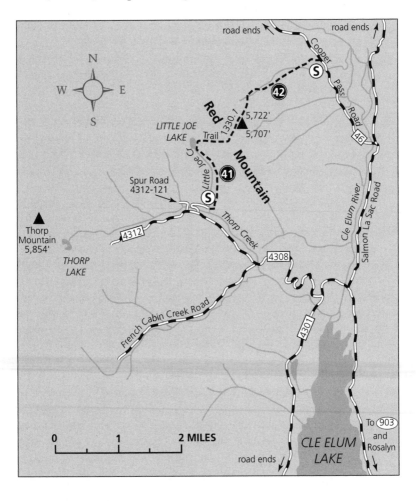

including Red Mountain Trail No. 1330.1, which is accessed from Little Joe Lake. Hikers looking for views and solitude will find them here.

Drive Interstate 90 east to the Roslyn exit, exit 80. Drive northwest on State Route 903 through the small town of Roslyn. From Roslyn drive northwest on the Salmon La Sac Road 12.5 miles and turn left on French Cabin Creek Road 4308, just past the end of Cle Elum Lake. Drive 3.2 miles, then turn right on Forest Road 4312 and drive about 1.5 miles; the roads are well signed. Look for a downhill road on the right-hand side, Spur Road 4312-121. The road is the beginning of the Thorp Creek Trail—the road may or may not be gated (if it's gated, proceed on foot). At 0.2 mile come to a junction—in 2000 there was a temporary sign for the Little Joe Lake Trail. Turn right and go less than 0.25 mile to a barricade at Little Joe Creek and the trailhead. There are no facilities.

Little Joe Lake Trail immediately crosses the creek (the only water source in late August), then climbs steeply, staying mostly in forest as it climbs. The trail is in good condition with only a few muddy sections and no blowdowns. The forest consists of Douglas fir, hemlock, grand fir, and spruce trees. In early summer the meadows and ridge crests are lush with flowers. By August most of the flowers have gone to seed and there is a tinge of fall color in the vine maple. At 1.75 miles reach Little Joe Lake (4,700 feet).

The sign for hiker-only Red Mountain Trail No. 1330.1 is nailed to a tree about halfway around the lake. The sign is not hard to locate, but you may have to scout around for the start of the trail because it begins in an area of pine forest where the ground is covered with pine needles and the tread is not obvious. Look for cut logs near the sign. Once you locate the start of the trail, it is fairly easy to follow and experienced hikers shouldn't have a problem with it.

The trail is faint in spots as it climbs through a blend of meadows and forest. A few side trails go off toward unknown destinations—these have been blocked with branches. A few helpful cairns and a few tactfully placed ribbons show the way (please do not add flags to the route). As the trail approaches the ridge crest, it becomes indistinct; continue uphill to find the trail again on the ridge crest. At about 2.25 miles, turn left to follow the trail about 0.25 mile to the site of the Red Mountain lookout at 5,707 feet.

There are several high points on Red Mountain that scramblers may wish to climb; use discretion, because some of the rocks are loose and there is some exposure. Experienced cross-country hikers with navigational skills may be able to arrange a one-way hike by descending the Red Mountain Trail (Hike 42) to Cooper Pass Road 46. This would

be approximately 6 miles one way, with potential routefinding challenges and a car shuttle.

42 RED MOUNTAIN VIA COOPER PASS ROAD

Distance: 7 miles round trip
Difficulty: Challenging
Type of trail: Maintained USFS trail
Starting point: 2,600 feet
High point: 5,707 feet, lookout site
Elevation gain: 3,107 feet
Hikable: Summer, fall
Maps: Green Trails No. 208 Kachess Lake; USGS Polallie Ridge
Information: Cle Elum Ranger District, 509-674-4411
Cautions: Stream crossings
See Hike 41 for map

Washington has many Red Mountains, but the Red Mountain Trail in Okanogan-Wenatchee National Forest near Salmon La Sac is not hiked as frequently as the other Red Mountain Trails. This seldom-hiked trail is described in the out-of-print *Teanaway Country* by Mary Sutliff (Signpost Publications, 1980), but does not appear in current hiking guides. Red Mountain is the site of an old lookout; the true summit is considered a scramble—most hikers stop short of the summit. The trail is scenic as it passes waterfalls and climbs to a lonely basin beneath the rocky ridge crest. Camping is possible in the basin and there is plenty of water nearby. A good time to experience the trail is in the fall before hunting season. The fall color should be spectacular because vine maple grows profusely along the trail; in late summer, berries are plentiful. Hikers and scramblers with cross-country hiking experience and routefinding skills enjoy exploring this trail.

Drive Interstate 90 east to the Roslyn/Salmon La Sac exit, exit 80. Drive northwest on State Route 903 through the small town of Roslyn. From Roslyn drive northwest on the Salmon La Sac Road about 15 miles, to Cooper Pass Road 46, and turn west on it. Drive just under 2 miles to the signed trailhead on the left. Find available parking off the road. There are no facilities.

A scrambler nears the summit of Red Mountain.

Hikers enjoying the view from the lookout site

The trail begins by climbing beside a stream and crosses a road before coming to a stream crossing at 0.75 mile. This can be a dangerous crossing and may necessitate a turnaround for some hikers if water is running high. Cross the creek and continue climbing as the trail switchbacks through forest until you meet a road that doesn't show on the 1986 Green Trails map. Find the trail again on the other side of the road. At about 2 miles (4,000 feet), the trail swings to the right and begins to head back toward the creek and another crossing of the stream that can also present a challenge early in the season.

The trail crosses a large talus slope and recrosses the creek at 4,300 feet. Here are good views down the valley and to distant peaks. The trail climbs and enters the basin at about 2.6 miles (4,600 feet). Good campsites are located near the stream at the head of the basin at 3 miles, above a marshy area interspersed with slide alder and boulders. This basin is just about as lonesome as you can get.

Scramblers can follow the ridge to the summit (5,722 feet) or continue 0.5 mile to the lookout site (5,707 feet). The trail beyond the basin may be obscure due to avalanche debris and blowdowns. When there is snow, ice axes are needed. The route climbs southwest and stays near the creek—look for faint tread or old blazes. Follow old tread along the ridge leading south to the lookout site and a connection to the unsigned Little Joe Lake Trail (Hike 41), which can be combined with this hike if you arrange a pickup or have two vehicles for a shuttle.

43 PARIS CREEK TRAIL

Distance: 6.6 miles round trip to North Fork Paris Creek Trail; 12.2 miles round trip to South Fork Boulder Creek Trail
Difficulty: Moderate
Type of trail: Old USFS road/occasionally maintained trail
Starting point: 2,800 feet
High point: 4,200 feet, North Fork Paris Creek trail junction; 5,800 feet, South Fork Boulder Creek trail junction
Elevation gain: 1,400 feet to North Fork Paris Creek trail junction; 3,000 feet to South Fork Boulder Creek trail junction
Hikable: Summer, fall
Maps: Green Trails No. 208 Kachess Lake, No. 209 Mount Stuart
Information: Cle Elum Ranger District, 509-674-4411
Cautions: Stream crossings, trail hard to follow in meadows, routefinding

Paris Creek Trail No. 1393.1 is a pleasant discovery in Okanogan-Wenatchee National Forest. Though it begins as a jeep road, in less than 0.13 mile it becomes a real trail in good condition. It is part of an old trail system in the Salmon La Sac district that follows along Paris Creek to seldom-visited basins and meadows. Paris Creek has three forks—the North, the Middle, and the South. When the snow melts, the meadows are a purple haze of shooting stars if you time it just right. The trail also has connections to several other trails in the Teanaway, including a spur to Jolly Mountain, the Middle Fork Teanaway trail, and the Boulder-DeRoux Trail (Hike 44). Several loops are feasible for hikers with navigation and routefinding skills—some of these trails are indistinct from lack of use and/or maintenance. Old trail signs may show different trail numbers from trails shown on current maps. Hikers and backpackers with routefinding skills enjoy scenery, wildlife, and camping.

Drive Interstate 90 east to the Roslyn exit, exit 80. Drive northwest on State Route 903 through the small town of Roslyn, and continue on Salmon La Sac Road along the Cle Elum lakeshore to the end of the county road, then turn right on Forest Road 4330 (Tucquala Lake Road). Continue 2 miles to the trailhead. This is also the trailhead and parking area for the popular Davis Peak Trail across the road to the north.

The Paris Creek Trail (Trail No. 1393.1) has recently been rerouted past an area of blowdowns and erosion (the old route followed more closely along Paris Creek). The trail levels, then rises to enter a clear-cut on a logging road at about 1.5 miles. The logging road is not shown on current maps. There is a small sign indicating "TRAIL" on a metal post at this spot. Turn right where the trail meets the road and hike about 0.13 mile to a road junction that may or may not be signed. Turn right and descend to the end of the road and resumption of trail (unsigned). The clear-cut is filling in with brush, serviceberry, and flowers. From the clear-cut, look back for a good view of Red Mountain to the west.

After crossing the creek, the trail continues through a forested area with dense vine maple. In June the ground is carpeted with vanilla leaf. At times you can see Paris Creek below as the trail stays

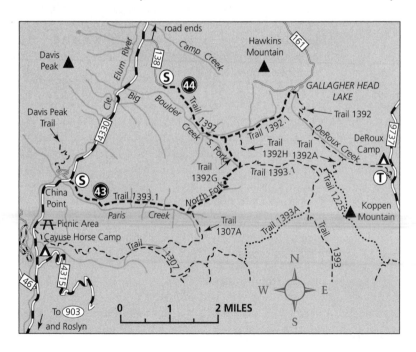

View from the Paris Creek Trail

above the creek. In early summer there are often patches of snow on the ground here and the trail may be difficult to follow. The trail descends to cross the creek at about 3 miles—there is no bridge. Look downstream a few feet for a log to cross on or hop and skip across (you may get a boot wet in the process). The trail continues a short distance to a trail junction at 3.3 miles. There are signs here but they are old and weathered, and may be confusing when compared with newer maps. From this junction the trail to the south (right) is a spur trail (Trail No. 1307A) up the South Fork of Paris Creek toward Jolly Mountain. The trail to the left follows the North Fork of Paris Creek. Many hikers turn around at this point.

Hikers with routefinding skills can follow the North Fork of Paris Creek 2.8 miles to the South Fork Boulder Creek Trail (Trail No. 1392G), which leads to the Boulder Creek Trail (part of Hike 44). (Note that the South Fork Boulder Creek Trail is shown as No. 1392G on the Green

Trails Mount Stuart map; in the *Cle Elum District Hiking Guide* it is designated as trail No. 1392.7. When map and trail numbers differ, study the map and you should be able to figure out which direction you need to go.)

From the junction at the end of the Paris Creek Trail, the North Fork of Paris Creek Trail switchbacks and climbs through forest near the creek. Several hunters' camps are passed along the way. The trail enters a large meadow that was a checkerboard of melting snow, shooting stars, and marsh marigolds in June. The meadows are very wet and fragile, and we could not pick up South Fork Boulder Creek Trail No. 1392G. According to the 1997 Green Trails map, Trail No. 1392G meets Boulder Creek Trail No. 1392 (Boulder-DeRoux Trail).

Strong hikers can make a loop trip by starting from Paris Creek and coming out at the Boulder Creek Trailhead or via Gallagher Head Lake to the DeRoux Trailhead (either of which would require a vehicle shuttle). Motorcycles are not allowed on the Paris Creek Trail or South Fork Boulder Creek Trail No. 1392G, but are allowed on the Boulder-DeRoux Trail.

Marsh marigolds

44 BOULDER-DEROUX TRAIL

Distance: 9.8 miles round trip to Gallagher Head Lake
Difficulty: Moderate
Type of trail: Maintained USFS trail
Starting point: 3,490 feet
High point: 4,600 feet, South Fork Boulder Creek Trail;
    5,600 feet, Gallagher Head Lake
Elevation gain: 1,110 feet to South Fork Boulder Creek
    Trail; 2,110 feet to Gallagher Head Lake
Hikable: Spring, summer, fall
Maps: Green Trails No. 209 Mount Stuart, No. 208 Kachess
    Lake; USGS Mount Stuart
Information: Cle Elum Ranger District, 509-674-4411
Cautions: Stream crossings, obsolete or missing trail signs,
    multi-use trail
See Hike 43 for map

Boulder-DeRoux Trail No. 1392 in Okanogan-Wenatchee National Forest is part of an old trail system with several trail connections. The Green Trails map shows many destinations worthy of a day hike or long backpacking loops. Some of these trails are open to motorcycles, and many of the trails are old and seldom hiked, with trailhead signs that may be missing and vague junctions. Many of these trails are unprotected, and conditions (including access) are subject to change. Experienced hikers enjoy the mining history, scenery, solitude, and camping. If you are unsure of your routefinding skills, you may be better off choosing one of the popular trails in the Alpine Lakes Wilderness from the Teanaway Road.

Boulder-DeRoux Trail No. 1392 has two trailheads; the most commonly used is the eastern trailhead accessed from the Teanaway Road 9737. The eastern trailhead is often described in hiking guides and so is not described here, but the western trailhead gets much less attention. The western trailhead (sometimes appearing on maps as the Boulder Creek Trail) is accessed from Salmon La Sac via Road 4330. The first mile of the road-trail crosses private property—in 2000 a hand-painted sign welcomed hikers but prohibited vehicles from driving to the end of the spur road where the trail begins. Because the spur road crosses private land, be respectful of any signage you encounter and don't trespass. If the trail appears closed, look for another hike nearby.

An unusual tree on the Boulder-DeRoux Trail

Because this approach to the trail is not described in hiking guides, the *Cle Elum Ranger District Hiking Guide* is strongly recommended. This handy guide can be purchased at the Cle Elum Ranger Station and outdoor equipment retail stores, or ordered from the Forest Service (see Appendix A).

Drive Interstate 90 to the Roslyn exit, exit 80. Drive northwest on

State Route 903 through the small town of Roslyn, and continue on Salmon La Sac Road along the Cle Elum lakeshore to the end of the county road, then turn right onto Forest Road 4330 (Tucquala Lake Road, also known as Fish Lake Road). Drive 5 miles and turn right on Spur Road 138. Drive about 0.25 mile on this steep, rough road and look for Spur Road 140 on your right (the road number is shown as 138 on the map). The road number may be missing, but there is a blank trailhead sign there. Park there, or if Road 140 is open, you may be able to drive to the end of the road, but parking is limited and conditions may change. If the road appears closed, park near the trailhead sign. There are no facilities. The trail begins from the end of the spur road, but because the spur road may be closed to vehicles, the hike is described from the beginning of the road.

The road climbs through scattered timber with views down to Boulder Creek. At 1 mile reach the end of the spur road, where no one should attempt to drive; the road becomes more trail-like as it rounds a ridge and enters the Boulder Creek canyon. You may feel as if you are walking on the moon. The terrain is desolate with few trees and the trail hugs steep walls of hardened earth embedded with rocks. The trail is narrow but in good condition as it crosses this rocky hillside. The trail descends slightly and then stays level for about 1 mile, at 2 miles crossing a small stream tumbling down on your left (Boulder Creek is on your right). This area is more heavily vegetated and there are ruins of cabins scattered throughout. The trail crosses Boulder Creek (this can be a difficult crossing in spring) and comes to a junction at 2.7 miles.

The Boulder-DeRoux Trail (Trail No. 1392.1), presently unsigned, continues straight; South Fork Boulder Creek Trail No. 1392G turns right. (Note that the South Fork Boulder Creek Trail is shown as No. 1392G on the Green Trails Mount Stuart map; in the *Cle Elum District Hiking Guide* it is designated as trail No. 1392.7. When map and trail numbers differ, study the map and you should be able to figure out which direction you need to go.) Both options are described here. Take the South Fork Boulder Creek Trail for a loop combined with the Paris Creek Trail (Hike 43). Take the Boulder-DeRoux Trail for a one-way hike to Gallagher Head Lake.

South Fork Boulder Creek Trail No. 1392G: Climb 600 feet in a gentle 1.2 miles to a large horse camp and the junction with Paris Creek Trail No. 1393.1 at 3.9 miles; this connection is vague. To the right the trail leads down to Paris Creek (Hike 43); to the left the trail climbs to a high point with views and other hiking options—in late August the flowers are past their prime, but many still bloom and the meadows are just starting to turn golden.

Boulder-DeRoux Trail No. 1392: Climb 0.3 mile to a junction with

Elsnor Mine Trail No. 1392H (also shown as No. 1392.8 on some maps) on the right at 3 miles. (The Elsnor Mine Trail, which may not be signed, climbs 0.8 mile close to the ruins of a historic mercury furnace.) Beyond the Elsnor Mine junction, the Boulder-DeRoux Trail (now shown as No. 1392.1 on some maps) continues climbing, ending in 1.9 miles at a junction with an off-road-vehicle road on the divide between Boulder and DeRoux Creeks at 4.9 miles. To continue to Gallagher Head Lake, follow the off-road-vehicle road a short distance to the lake. Quiet camps are a short distance below the lake in a large meadow on the Boulder-DeRoux Trail.

45 JUNGLE CREEK TRAIL

Distance: 7-mile loop; 8.4 miles round trip to Malcolm Mountain
Difficulty: Moderate
Type of trail: Occasionally maintained USFS trail
Starting point: 3,000 feet
High point: 4,800 feet, loop; 5,840 feet, Malcolm Mountain
Elevation gain: 1,800 feet on loop; 2,840 to Malcolm Mountain
Hikable: Spring, summer, fall
Map: Green Trails No. 209 Mount Stuart
Information: Cle Elum Ranger District, 509-674-4411
Cautions: Routefinding, game trails, confusion with old/new trail signs

Many hiking trails in the Teanaway district of Okanogan-Wenatchee National Forest are featured in current hiking guides. However, Jungle Creek Trail No. 1383A (shown on some maps as 1383.1) is not described in hiking guides, slipping into obscurity. This trail connects to several other trails in the district, and the Green Trails Mount Stuart map illustrates several loops that are possible. Even elusive Malcolm Mountain can be reached from this trail, though the path is faint and confusing. New trail signs have been placed and some of the trails have new numbers that might not coincide with older maps. Be sure to take a compass.

The Teanaway country is so sublimely beautiful that just about anyplace you stop is good enough to be called "destination." The ridges are long with many viewpoints and whether or not they have a name may not be terribly important. If you don't get as far as Malcolm or

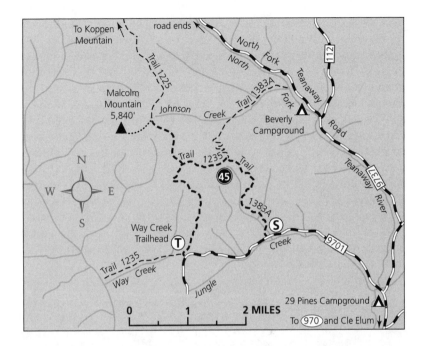

Koppen Mountain (Trail No. 1225), you'll still have a full day. The Jungle Creek Trail is open to stock as well as motorcycles. It is a multiple-use trail but it doesn't seem to get much use and you might not encounter anyone. Naturalists are familiar with this trail as a source of unusual wildflowers early in the year, but by midsummer many of the flowers are gone. In late spring the lower elevations of trail are vibrant with yellow violets, calypso orchids, phacelia, and flowering currant.

Drive Interstate 90 to State Route 970 east of Cle Elum, and in 5 miles turn left on Teanaway Road. In about 7.5 miles turn right on North Fork Teanaway Road 9737, following it about 6 miles to 29 Pines Campground. Turn left on gravel Jungle Creek Road 9701 and drive 2.4 bumpy miles to the signed trailhead on the right. There is room at the trailhead for three or four cars. There are no facilities.

Follow Trail 1383A for 0.5 mile to a stream crossing where lupine, luina, and gooseberry are seen. The trail crosses the stream several times, but none of the crossings are difficult. At about 1 mile the trail climbs away from the creek—this steep section is badly eroded. At about 2 miles the trail breaks out into the open with views of Johnson Peak (5,200 feet), a nontechnical peak with a scramble route to the top. The trail goes around a rocky outcropping—a good setting for Indian paintbrush, death camas, and stonecrop. Another steep 0.25 mile leads to the ridge crest at 2.2 miles and a junction (4,500 feet). Trail names have changed and signs may be in place showing both the old and new names—this may create some confusion. In the past the Johnson-Medra Trail was shown as a loop, but sections have been renamed or combined with Koppen Mountain Trail No. 1225, Way Creek Trail No. 1235, and Jungle Creek Trail No. 1383A. The Jungle Creek Trail continues west along the ridge, but is now signed as the Way Creek Trail (Trail No. 1235). At this junction there are plenty of logs to sit on, take a break, and study the map.

From the junction, go left on the Jungle Creek Trail as it becomes the Way Creek Trail, continuing a mile along the north side of the ridge to a high point (4,800 feet). A short distance beyond the high point, the trail comes to the Koppen Mountain junction at 3.2 miles (approximately 4,800 feet). From there the Way Creek Trail goes left to descend to Jungle Creek Road and the Koppen Mountain Trail goes to the right.

A spring scramble of Johnson Peak

Jungle Creek–Way Creek Loop: To hike a loop, follow the Way Creek Trail south as it drops through forest a couple miles (you may encounter a Jeep or motorcycle) to the Way Creek Trailhead on the deeply rutted Jungle Creek Road at 5.3 miles (3,600 feet). It is another 1.7 miles along the road to the Jungle Creek Trailhead at 7 miles.

Malcolm Mountain: Turn right on the Koppen Mountain Trail and continue along the ridge until you reach a ridge running north at an elevation of 4,800 feet, the southern end of an old sheep driveway. Hike along the ridge about a mile and follow vague tread north, then west to the summit of Malcolm Mountain at 4.2 miles (5,840 feet). Map, compass, and altimeter are all necessary here because many faint trails intersect each other and you cannot depend on signs. (To save 1 mile and 600 feet of elevation gain, begin from the Way Creek Trailhead for a shorter route to Malcolm Mountain.)

46 STANDUP CREEK TRAIL

Distance: 8.5 miles round trip
Difficulty: Challenging
Type of trail: USFS, maintained
Starting point: 3,100 feet
High point: 6,200 feet
Elevation gain: 3,100 feet
Hikable: Summer, fall
Maps: Green Trails No. 209 Mount Stuart; USGS Red Top Mountain, Enchantment Lakes
Information: Cle Elum Ranger District, 509-674-4411
Cautions: Routefinding, stream crossings

Though Standup Creek Trail No. 1369 in Okanogan-Wenatchee National Forest appears in older hiking guides, it does not get as much use as other trails in the area. Standup Creek Road 112 that accesses the trailhead is rough, not recommended for passenger cars, and sometimes impassable even to vehicles with high clearance, adding a 1.5-mile road walk. Hikers often choose to park at the Standup Creek road junction on Stafford Creek Road 9703 and hike to the trailhead to spare their cars. In addition to the challenge of getting to the trailhead, hikers face multiple crossings of Standup Creek. The hike is best done in mid-summer after spring melt-off when stream crossings are easier.

In 1999 hikers witnessed the devastation left by an avalanche resulting from the heavy snowfall during the severe winter of 1998–1999. Hikers were awed by the damage the avalanche had done to the gentle Teanaway. The avalanche took out many trees as it roared down the Standup Creek drainage. The images would have served well as textbook pictures depicting the effects of avalanche, with trees snapped in half and old chunks of dirty snow choking the gullies. By 1999 hikers had made detours around the debris that blocked the trail, and today few traces remain. The high ridges in the Teanaway can also be dangerous in spring and early summer because thunderstorms frequently boil up in the afternoons on the eastern side of the Cascades. Be sure to get an up-to-date weather forecast and keep an eye on the sky.

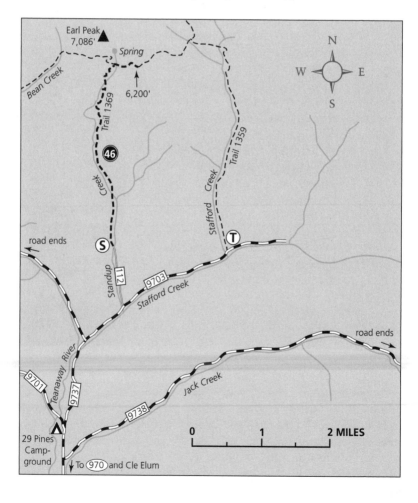

Earl Peak

Standup Creek Trail No. 1369 is an easy approach to Earl Peak (7,086 feet), considered a walk-up by regular scramblers. Earl Peak can also be accessed from Bean Basin, and a look at the Green Trails Mount Stuart map shows several possible loops within this region. In general the Standup Creek Trail is easier to follow than it was years ago when it simply vanished in a meadow beneath Earl Peak. The trail system is better signed these days, but it is still lonesome country from Standup Creek to the junction with the more popular Stafford Creek Trail No. 1359 (your best bet for solitude is the Standup Creek Trail). Today the Standup Creek Trail is passable all the way to the 6,200-foot saddle on the ridge crest and is suitable for most hikers. Hikers, backpackers, and scramblers enjoy views, easy access to Earl Peak, and links to other trails.

Drive Interstate 90 to State Route 970 east of Cle Elum, and in 5 miles turn left on Teanaway Road. In about 7.5 miles turn right on North Fork Teanaway Road 9737, following it about 6 paved miles to 29 Pines Campground. Continue on the Teanaway Road (it becomes a dirt road) and drive 1.5 miles to signed Stafford Creek Road 9703. Turn right and drive a long mile to Standup Creek Spur Road 112 (2,800 feet). Park at the road junction or drive at your discretion—it is a long mile to the Standup Creek Trailhead.

The trail begins as an old road following along Standup Creek. At about 1 mile it makes the first of five creek crossings as it makes a gentle climb up the valley. By mid- to late summer, none of the crossings are difficult. At about 3.5 miles it makes the last of the five stream crossings. The trail ascends through a meadow to a signed junction below the crest of the ridge. A trail to Bean Creek basin goes left; recent reports indicate that the trail to Bean Creek is vague and may be hard to follow (look for cairns). Continue on the Standup Creek/Stafford Creek Trail to the right.

Beyond the junction, the Standup Creek Trail enters forest and climbs to a high point of 6,200 feet on the crest of the ridge at about 4.25 miles with views to the south. This is a gorgeous spot and the obvious stopping place for lunch before turning around.

Hikers with cross-country hiking skills find Earl Peak an easy scramble from the saddle—simply follow the ridge northwest to the summit about 0.75 mile (7,086 feet). Backpackers or strong hikers can make a loop by continuing from the ridge crest on the Standup Creek Trail, dropping from the saddle into a large basin. The route is vague and trailfinding skills come in handy. There are several campsites in the basin near the creek and small lakes that are not shown on maps. The trail descends to meet the Stafford Creek Trail (Trail No. 1359) at 5.9 miles (5,000 feet), following it 4.8 miles to the Stafford Creek Road at 10.7 miles one way. You will have to leave another car at the Stafford Creek Trailhead, about 1.5 miles from the Standup Creek road junction, or walk the road to close the loop.

Hikers on the trail to Noble Knob

MOUNT RAINIER AND STATE ROUTE 410

47 CHENUIS FALLS TRAIL

Distance: 3 miles round trip
Difficulty: Moderate
Type of trail: Maintained NPS trail/abandoned USFS trail
Starting point: 2,160 feet
High point: 3,160 feet
Elevation gain: 1,000 feet
Hikable: Summer, fall
Map: USGS Mowich Lake
Information: Mount Rainier National Park Wilkeson
   Wilderness Information Center, 360-829-5127
Cautions: Blowdowns, routefinding

It is hard to find out much information about this trail. It does not show on Forest Service or Green Trails maps. A few who know of it wryly refer to this easy-to-hike trail as the "nontrail." It was sometimes called the North Boundary Trail (the first mile of the trail is within Mount Rainier National Park). The Park Service is aware of the trail, but it is not on its list of maintained trails. This is primarily because most of the trail is not in the park and because it doesn't go anywhere. This was one of the last trails the Civilian Conservation Corps (CCC) worked on in the park before the second world war. The trail would have ended at Hurricane Gap, but World War II ended the trail project. There was a work camp in the area called Gunnysack Camp that only a few locals know how to locate. The trail (or a branch of it) may have led to Chenuis Mountain. Chenuis Mountain did not have a lookout, but there was a lookout near Windy Gap on Windy Knoll, which is at the head of the Chenuis Creek drainage.

If you are wondering what the payoff is—it's the trees. This is absolutely some of the finest old growth we've seen. Some of the Douglas firs must be at least 800 years old. Where there are no trees, gentle moss covers the trail and wildflowers abound. Who needs views? Besides, you do get a stunning view of Mount Rainier as you cross the Carbon River near the Chenuis Falls Trailhead.

The Carbon River runs amok every winter, often washing out the Carbon River Road and the beginning of the Chenuis Falls Trail. Bridges over the Carbon River are put in each year by the park rangers who maintain the trail as far as Chenuis Falls (a worthy destination itself). Beyond Chenuis Falls the trail is not maintained except for the volunteer

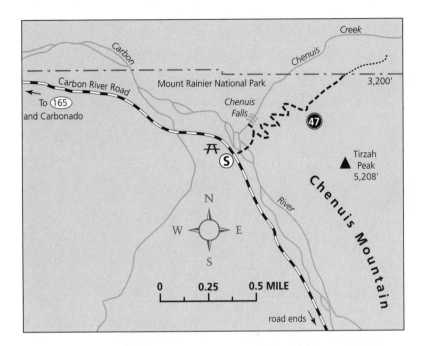

efforts of hikers who are familiar with it. On summer weekends Chenuis Falls is a crowded place with families, tourists, and hikers wanting an easy trip. Most of them don't know there is more—so much more. Climbers and scramblers with routefinding skills can travel cross-country to several high points on Chenuis Mountain (Tirzah Peak at 5,208 feet is one) or look for Chenuis Lakes. However, most hikers should stay on the trail because venturing off trail involves brush, blowdowns, and cross-country navigation on steep hillsides and cliffs. We have not hiked the entire trail, but it continues 3 miles beyond the park boundary and is said to end a couple hundred yards from a clear-cut. The road to the clear-cut is about 300 yards up the hill, but the logging road has washed out and is apparently no longer accessible. Hikers with routefinding skills enjoy solitude and old-growth forest.

From Interstate 5 or 405 near Renton, drive south on State Route 167 to SR 410 in Sumner. Drive east on SR 410 to Buckley, then south on SR 165 through Wilkeson and Carbonado. In 3 miles south of Carbonado the road forks: SR 165 (the Mowich Road) goes to the right; turn left onto the Carbon River Road and drive 9 miles to the Carbon River entrance of Mount Rainier National Park (entrance fee required). From the entrance continue 3.6 miles to the signed

Crossing the Carbon River

trailhead on the left. There is room for several cars. Trailhead facilities consist of picnic tables.

Follow the sandy path bordered by stones to a series of footbridges over the Carbon River. This is also your best chance to get a view of Mount Rainier. Enter the forest, cross a stream on a bridge, and in 0.3 mile reach the signed spur trail to a viewpoint of Chenuis Falls.

For more experienced hikers, this is just the start of an interesting journey. Beyond the sign for Chenuis Falls, the abandoned trail to the right/straight ahead is easy to spot as it continues to climb through old-growth forest. The trail is in good condition for the first mile or so beyond the falls. Only a few minor blowdowns litter the wide, easy path and these are easily stepped over or around. The forest is old, dark, and peaceful, and where there are not colossal trees, mosses and ferns glitter with morning dew. Through the trees are glimpses of cliff bands and random boulders. One giant fir along the trail must measure at least 8 to 10 feet in diameter—there are several of these giants safely within the boundary of the park.

The trail switchbacks up 1,000 feet in about 0.75 mile, leveling off and coming to the signed park boundary at 1.2 miles. The old growth is spectacular, and deer moss carpets the ground. The trail remains in fairly good condition for another 0.3 mile or so beyond the park boundary. There are more blowdowns, but there are no obstacles difficult enough to stop seasoned hikers. The trail crosses a couple of boggy sections where little streams come in from the right. These probably dry up later in the summer.

The trail comes to a high point (gain about 1,000 feet from the trailhead) and comes to a vague and unsigned junction (about 3,200 feet). A vague trail heads uphill, but it doesn't appear to go anywhere. The main trail descends slightly and soon becomes more difficult. A big tree (one of several) blocks the trail and it is a struggle to get around. You can squeeze under it or go around, but it is messy. This is followed by more blowdowns, and the tread narrows as young firs are filling in the trail. We turned around at approximately 0.3 mile from the park boundary, 1.5 miles from the trailhead.

48 NOBLE KNOB VIA DALLES RIDGE

Distance: 4.2 miles round trip to Noble Knob
Difficulty: Moderate
Type of trail: Maintained USFS trail
Starting point: 5,300 feet
High point: 6,011 feet
Elevation gain: 711 feet
Hikable: Summer, fall
Maps: Green Trails No. 238 Greenwater, No. 239 Lester
Information: Snoqualmie Ranger District (Enumclaw), 360-825-6585; Mount Rainier National Park, 360-569-2211
Cautions: None

Noble Knob is the site of a forest fire lookout and a high point with calendar-type views of Mount Rainier that you can get to earlier in the hiking season than other popular destinations in the high country. There are several approaches for Noble Knob, including the well-known Noble Knob Trail No. 1184; the most popular is the Corral Pass approach in Norse Peak Wilderness (described in other hiking guides). The Corral Pass approach is straightforward but crowded during the prime hiking season. For more solitude the Dalles Ridge route is the preferred approach. The Dalles Ridge Trail No. 1173 doesn't get a lot of

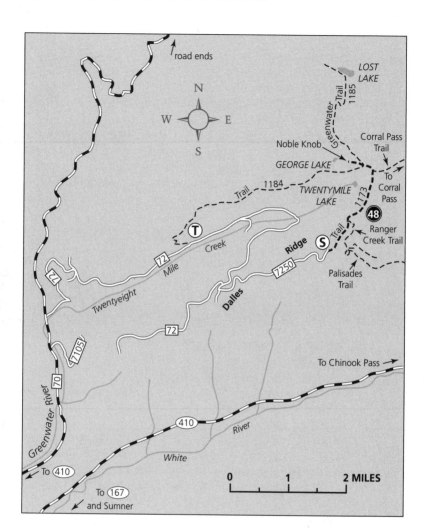

attention from the public, though the trail in Mount Baker–Snoqualmie National Forest is maintained and in good condition. The most challenging aspect of this route is finding the trailhead. Though the Green Trails maps are helpful, they are not always up to date because conditions are constantly changing due to road washouts and logging activity. Call the Snoqualmie Ranger District for current road conditions before setting out. In 2000 the roads were in good condition and the trailhead was signed. The Dallas Ridge Trail connects with the Ranger Creek Trail and the Palisades Trail—you can conceivably hike all the way down to State Route 410 on these trails for a one-way hike if you have a vehicle shuttle.

From Interstate 5 or 405 near Renton, drive south on State Route 167 to SR 410 in Sumner. Drive east on SR 410 through Enumclaw and Greenwater, then continue east, turning left onto paved Forest Road 70. Pass Forest Road 7015 to the right and, just past a big U-turn on Road 70, turn right onto Forest Road 72 (Twentyeight Mile Road). In about 4 miles from Forest Road 70, the trailhead for Noble Knob Trail No. 1184 is on the left (hikers wanting more of a workout could start here, as described in other guidebooks). Continue on Road 72—a cliffhanger—and at about 8 miles from Road 70, turn left on Forest Road 7250. Pass a signed viewpoint and continue to a three-way junction. Take the middle

Hikers on the Noble Knob Trail

road and drive about 2 miles to the end of that road and the trailhead signed "DALLES RIDGE." There are no facilities here.

Follow the Dalles Ridge Trail (Trail No. 1173) as climbs 200 feet in 0.5 mile to the junction with the Ranger Creek Trail on the right, which descends to State Route 410. Stay left on the Dalles Ridge Trail as it follows along and near the top of a ridge. On a foggy day you won't see much, but early summer flowers compensate. Beargrass, snowdrops, lupine, and penstemon can brighten a gloomy day. If the day is fair, you'll see Noble Knob coming into view on your left. Look down on your right for glimpses of the White River and the foothills of Enumclaw.

At 1.5 miles the trail reaches another junction (5,600 feet). To the right is the main trail coming in from Corral Pass; continue straight. The trail contours beneath the ridge and climbs 100 feet to another junction in 0.2 mile, 1.7 miles from your start. To the right is Lost Lake via the Greenwater Trail No. 1185; (another trail descends to a lake). Continue straight ahead.

Follow along the ridge 0.4 mile toward Noble Knob. From this point, it is a flower garden the rest of the way. The terrain is open and scenic with only a few clumps of subalpine trees here and there. The ground cover is lush with spreading phlox, penstemon, stonecrop, and larkspur; a few white snags add drama to the scene. The trail climbs 300 feet around Noble Knob and spirals to the top at 2.1 miles, with many places to sit and enjoy the vistas.

Because this is not a strenuous hike, consider more options. If the weather is not conducive to basking on the summit, backtrack 1.6 miles on the Dalles Ridge Trail to the junction with Ranger Creek Trail No. 1197. Descend about 300 feet in 1 mile on good trail to a shelter (built by Boy Scouts) at 4.7 miles, an excellent place for lunch on a cold or drizzly day. The trail to the Palisades takes off from here as well. The Ranger Creek Trail continues 3 miles to a viewpoint of Ranger Peak at 7.7 miles, and descends to SR 410 in another 3 miles, 10.7 miles total one way (including the jaunt to Noble Knob).

49 DEADWOOD LAKES

> **Distance: 2.2 miles round trip**
> **Difficulty:** Moderate
> **Type of trail:** Abandoned NPS trail
> **Starting point:** 5,430 feet
> **High point:** 5,600 feet
> **Elevation gain:** 170 feet in; 300 feet out
> **Hikable:** Summer, fall
> **Maps:** Green Trails No. 270 Mt. Rainier East; USGS White
>   River
> **Information:** Mount Rainier National Park, 360-569-2211;
>   Wenatchee National Forest (Naches), 509-653-2205
> **Cautions:** None

The two small Deadwood Lakes are located just inside the boundary of Mount Rainier National Park, nestled in a landscape of meadows interspersed with forest. This area is buggy in summer months. September is an excellent time to hike here when huckleberries grow profusely along the trail and the meadows are full of blue gentians. By September most of the bugs are gone except for a few bees bumbling about doing their last-minute getting-ready-for-winter business. Elk frequent these meadows—if the elk droppings are fresh, the elk are not far away.

This trail has dropped out of hiking guidebooks, but it is still in good condition for those with trailfinding skills who enjoy solitude.

Several scenic and easy hikes that are often crowded are located where the Pacific Crest Trail No. 2000 crosses Chinook Pass. Hikers who take the time to look at old maps or guidebooks relish discovering such a gem as Deadwood Lakes. According to the National Park Service, the trail was never a formally constructed and maintained trail (it's not shown on maps). It has become a way trail developed by hikers and

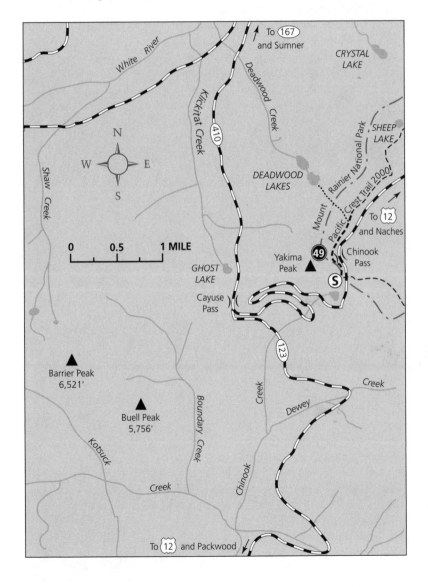

fishermen. There are several abandoned trails in and near Mount Rainier National Park. At one time there were several routes to the mountain used by Native Americans; some of those were also used by early explorers and settlers. Native Americans trails were not specific trails as much as routes that varied as conditions changed. They didn't maintain trails, so if trees blew down across the trail or the snow didn't melt out, they moved the route to go around the obstacle.

Because the trail is no longer maintained, the park's cross-country travel regulations apply. Sections of the trail that are not within the park are administered by the Wenatchee National Forest. Deadwood Lakes themselves lie within the park; a backcountry permit must be obtained for all overnight backcountry camping, but is not required for day hikes. There are no campsites on the lakeshore (camping near water is prohibited anyway), but there is a primitive campsite between the two lakes in forest that is probably far enough away from the water to be within regulations. Mount Rainier National Park does not encourage backcountry hiking and camping; they prefer to send people to designated camping areas, though hiking on abandoned trails within the park is not prohibited. Be sure to follow all rules and regulations that apply to backcountry hiking and camping.

From Interstate 5 or 405 near Renton, drive south on State Route 167 to SR 410 in Sumner. Drive east on SR 410 through Enumclaw and and continue east to Chinook Pass. Drive under the "overpass" and park on the east side of the summit in a parking area with restrooms. Parking is not a problem midweek in September; a weekend in August may be a different story. If the parking lot is full, another parking area is a little farther east. In early September the restroom was already "closed for the winter," but portable toilets remain in place.

The hike begins on the well-signed Pacific Crest Trail No. 2000 near the overpass. Set your altimeter to 5,430 feet—the reading at Chinook Pass. Follow the PCT north above State Route 410 until you lose about 100 feet in elevation. In about 0.6 mile look for an unsigned trail climbing uphill on your left. A few feet beyond this trail, another trail also goes uphill—this trail is blocked with brush and small trees that make it stand out. Either one of the two trails works. The two trails join in a few feet and gently climb about 0.2 mile through a corridor of huckleberry bushes to a saddle at about 0.8 mile (about 5,600 feet) between two peaks. Here you enter Mount Rainier National Park.

Deadwood Lake

The trail descends about 360 feet over 0.3 mile through forest and meadows; the lakes come into view as you descend. Though the trail is not maintained, it is easy to follow until you get to the meadows around the lakes at about 1.1 miles (5,236 feet). Game trails and lush vegetation make routefinding a bit confusing, but unless it is foggy you can find your way without difficulty. Follow the trail if you can—it dips close to the first lake and crosses a wet meadow before reentering forest. If you lose the trail, look for the best game trail—there are many to choose from. The two lakes are separated by a forested strip of land. The first lake has an outlet stream that flows into the second, shallower lake; the very serene lake has a sandy bottom. This lake makes a good lunch spot because the sandy shore has dry logs to sit on.

50 MEEKS TABLE

Distance: Approximately 4 miles round trip
Difficulty: Moderate
Type of trail: Old road/abandoned USFS trail
Starting point: 4,000 feet
High point: 4,400 feet
Elevation gain: 400 feet
Hikable: Spring, summer, fall
Maps: Green Trails No. 272 Old Scab Mountain, No. 273
    Manastash Lake
Information: Naches Ranger District, 509-653-2205
Cautions: Trailhead unsigned, hard to find

You'll have to search high and low for information on this trail. Meeks Table appears on Green Trails maps, but the Naches Ranger District is probably your best source of information. The Forest Service does not prohibit hiking here, but they would like this trail to keep a low profile and are not actively encouraging hikers. Ask about Meeks Table Research Natural Area (RNA) and the condition of access roads. This is a sensitive environmental area just inside the William O. Douglas Wilderness, and party size should be kept to a minimum. Because Meeks Table has never been commercially grazed by sheep or cattle, it has become an interesting ecological area to study. Meeks Table is also home to stands of old-growth pine. Several research papers have been written about this plateau.

The best time to visit Meeks Table is in May and June when the flowers are blooming, but be sure the roads are snowfree before you set

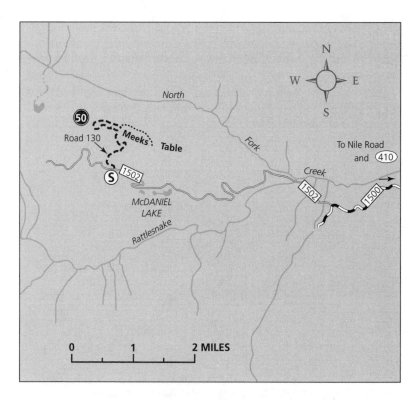

out. In June we saw many varieties of wildflowers (some rarely seen), including spreading phlox, death camas, bitterroot, balsamroot, lomatium, buckwheat, phacelia, lupine, penstemons (including shrubby penstemon), columbia lily (not yet in bloom), fleabane, bitterbrush, Thompson's paintbrush (white), luina, alumroots (heuchera), geum (old man's whiskers), saxifrage, sandwort, pussytoes, arnica, stonecrop (not in bloom), and yarrow. Earlier in the season, grass widows can be seen. The most unusual plant you may encounter is giant frasera, which can grow to 7 feet and is very showy. If you come across one, consider it a privilege and take only pictures. Hikers and naturalists enjoy wildflowers, the area's geology, and views. Watch for rattlesnakes and ticks. Carry water; Meeks Table is dry. Camping and fires are prohibited.

From Interstate 5 or 405 near Renton, drive south on State Route 167 to SR 410 in Sumner. Drive east on SR 410 through Enumclaw and continue east to Chinook Pass; reset your odometer to 0. Continue east on SR 410 26.5 miles to the small community of Cliffdell. Continue east; at 34.9 miles bypass Nile Road 1600 and continue to Nile Road

1500 at 38.5 miles (milepost 108). The Wood Shed Restaurant is located at this road junction. Turn right onto Road 1500; at all junctions, stay left on Road 1500 and cross a bridge at 41.2 miles. Continue going west on paved Road 1500. There are signs pointing the way to McDaniel Lake. At the end of the pavement at 47.7 miles, turn right onto Road 1502, passing McDaniel Lake and continuing less than 2 miles to a metal post at Spur Road 130. The spur road may be too rough for pas-

Meeks Table

senger cars—if so, park along the shoulder of Road 1502. The 0.25-mile spur road is easily hiked. If you continue on Spur Road 130, park on a wide grassy area on your right or a little beyond at the end of the spur and a turnaround with room for a few vehicles. There is no trailhead sign for Meeks Table and the trail register described in old hiking guides has been removed.

From the end of the spur road, look for a rough road heading uphill to the right. This is the continuation of Road 130, but the road has been bermed. The track climbs a short distance through shrubs and becomes trail. Though there are no signs, the trail is easy to follow as it climbs west in loose talus. At about 1 mile the way veers sharply right (east) along the wilderness boundary. After a short climb, at about 2 miles the trail enters a large flat plateau—Meeks Table—covered with grasses and stands of ponderosa pine. The butte is a mile long and you can circumnavigate it or hike as far as you wish. If hiking counterclockwise, the cliffs to your right (south) are Bethel Ridge, and McDaniel Lake can be seen from this side of the plateau as well.

APPENDIX A: RESOURCES

Custom Correct Maps
c/o Little River Enterprises
3492 Little River Road
Port Angeles, WA 98363
www.olypen.com/lre

Green Trails, Inc.
P.O. Box 77734
Seattle, WA 98177
206-546-6277
http://greentrailsmaps.com

Outdoor Recreation Information
  Center (at REI)
222 Yale Avenue North
Seattle, WA 98109-5429
206-470-4060

USGS Maps
*http://mcmcweb.er.usgs.gov/
  topomaps/ordering_maps.html*

LAND MANAGEMENT
AGENCIES
**Mount Baker–Snoqualmie
  National Forest**
21905 64th Avenue West
Mountlake Terrace, WA 98043
425-775-9702

**Mount Baker–Snoqualmie
  National Forest Ranger Districts**
Darrington Ranger District
1405 Emons Street
Darrington, WA 98241
360-436-1155

Enumclaw Public Service Center
450 Roosevelt Avenue East
Enumclaw, WA 98022
360-825-6585

Mount Baker District
2105 State Route 20
Sedro-Woolley, WA 98284
360-856-5700

Skykomish District
74920 Northeast Stevens Pass
  Highway
P.O. Box 305
Skykomish, WA 98288
360-677-2414

Snoqualmie District
42404 Southeast North Bend
  Way
North Bend, WA 98045
425-888-1421

Rainforest, Olympic Mountains

Verlot Public Service Center
33515 Mountain Loop Highway
Granite Falls, WA 98252
360-691-7791 (summer only)

Okanogan National Forest
Co-located with Wenatchee
    National Forest headquarters
Okanogan Valley Office
1240 Second Avenue South
Okanogan, WA 98840-9723
509-662-4335

**Okanogan and Wenatchee
    National Forests**
215 Melody Lane
Wenatchee, WA 98801-5933
509-826-3275

**Wenatchee National Forest
    Ranger Districts**
Cle Elum Ranger District
803 West Second Street
Cle Elum, WA 98922
509-674-4411

Lake Wenatchee Ranger District
22976 State Route 207
Leavenworth, WA 98826
509-763-3103

Leavenworth Ranger District
600 Sherbourne
Leavenworth, WA 98826
509-548-6977

Methow Valley Ranger District
P.O. Box 188
502 Glover
Twisp, WA 98856
509-997-2131

Naches Ranger District
10061 U.S. Highway 12
Naches, WA 98937
509-653-2205

Olympic National Forest
1835 Black Lake Boulevard
    Southwest
Olympia, WA 98512-5623
360-956-2300

**Olympic National Forest Ranger
    Districts**
Hood Canal Ranger District
Hoodsport Office
150 North Lake Cushman Road
P.O. Box 68
Hoodsport, WA 98548
360-877-5254

Pacific Ranger District
Quinault Office
353 South Shore Road
P.O. Box 9
Quinault, WA 98575
360-288-2525

Mount Rainier National Park
Mail: Tahoma Woods
Star Route
Ashford, WA 98304-9751
360-569-2211 (headquarters)
Fax: 360-569-2170
Email: *MORAinfo@nps.gov*

North Cascades National Park
Mail: 2105 State Route 20
Sedro-Woolley, WA 98284-9394
360-856-5700 (headquarters)
Fax: 360-856-5700
Email:
NOCA_Interpretation@nps.gov

Olympic National Park
Mail: 600 East Park Avenue
Port Angeles, WA 98362-6798
360-565-3130 (visitor
    information), 360-565-3131
    (recorded message)
Fax: 360-565-3147
Email: *olym_Olympic_park-
    vc@nps.gov*

OTHER RESOURCES

Hikers who would like to volunteer to work on trails can contact the organizations listed below:

Alpine Lakes Protection Society
    (ALPS)
100 98th Avenue, Suite E-6
Bellevue, WA 98004-5401
http://members.aol.com/alpineLPS

Issaquah Alps Trails Club
P.O. Box 122
Issaquah, WA 98027
www.issaquahalps.org

Mid-Forc
P.O. Box 25809
Seattle, WA 98125-1309

Pacific Northwest Trail
    Association
P.O. Box 1817
Mount Vernon, WA 98273
877-854-9415
www.pnt.org

Sierra Club, Cascade Chapter
8511 15th Avenue Northeast,
    Suite 201
Seattle, WA 98115
206-523-2147
Fax: 206-729-2468
www.cascadechapter.org

Snoqualmie Valley Trails Club
P.O. Box 1741
North Bend, WA 97202

Washington Trails Association
1305 Fourth Avenue, Room 512
Seattle, WA 98101
206-625-1367
www.wta.org

Washington Wilderness
    Coalition
4649 Sunnyside Avenue North
Seattle, WA 98103
206-633-1992
Fax: 206-633-1996
www.wawild.org

APPENDIX B:
SELECTED READING

All of The Mountaineers Books hiking guides, including *Footloose* and *Footsore* series, past to present.

Beckey, Fred. *Cascade Alpine Guide: Columbia River to Stevens Pass.* 3rd ed. Vol. 1. Seattle: The Mountaineers Books, 2000.

———. *Cascade Alpine Guide: Stevens Pass to Rainy Pass.* Vol. 2. Seattle: The Mountaineers Books, 1996.

———. *Cascade Alpine Guide: Rainy Pass to Fraser River.* Vol. 3. Seattle: The Mountaineers Books, 1995.

Chang, Ina, ed. *Discovering Washington's Historic Mines.* Vol. 1. Arlington, Wash.: Oso Publishing, 1997.

Crowder, D. F., and R. W. Tabor. *Routes and Rocks—Hikers Guide to the North Cascades from Glacier Peak to Lake Chelan.* Seattle: The Mountaineers Books, 1965.

Dreisbach, Bob. *Seattle Outdoors.* Kenmore, Wash.: Entropy Conservationists, 2000.

Dreisbach, Carl. *Middle Fork Guide: Seattle's Closest Mountains.* Vashon Island, Wash.: Big Raven Book, 1997.

Majors, Harry, and Richard McCollum. *Monte Cristo Area: A Complete Outdoor Guide.* Seattle: Northwest Press, 1977.

The Mountaineers. *The Mountaineer Annual.* Vol. 11. Seattle: The Mountaineers, 1918. All other volumes to present as well.

Kresek, Ray. *Fire Lookouts of the Northwest.* 3rd ed. Spokane, Wash.: Historic Lookout Project, 1998.

Parratt, Smitty. *Gods & Goblins.* Port Angeles, Wash.: CP Publications, 1984.

Spring, Ira, and Harvey Manning. *100 Hikes in Washington's Glacier Peak Region: The North Cascades.* 3rd ed. Seattle: The Mountaineers Books, 1996.

Sutliff, Mary. *Teanaway Guide.* Lynnwood, Wash.: Signpost Publications, 1980.

———. *Entiat Country.* Lynnwood, Wash.: Signpost Publications, 1985.

Wood, Robert L. *Olympic Mountains Trail Guide*. 3rd ed. Seattle: The Mountaineers Books, 2000.

Woodhouse, Philip. *Monte Cristo*. Seattle: The Mountaineers Books, 1979.

INDEX

ABOUT THE AUTHOR

Karen Sykes is a freelance writer whose column "Hike of the Week" appears weekly in the "Getaways" section of the *Seattle Post-Intelligencer*. She has been an active volunteer with the Mountaineers Club, serving as the chairperson of the Hiking Committee for one year, the chair of the Snowshoe Committee for three years, and the chair of the Alpine Scramble Committee for two years. She has led hikes for the Mountaineers Club since 1982 and also has taken groups on scrambling and snow-shoeing trips. She is also a member of the Washington Trails Association (WTA). Two books of her poetry have been published, both under her previous name Karen Waring: *Exposed to the Elements* was published by Litmus Press of Salt Lake City, Utah, and *A Child's Poem and Other Poems* was published by Open Skull Press of Sacramento, California.

THE MOUNTAINEERS, founded in 1906, is a nonprofit outdoor activity and conservation club, whose mission is "to explore, study, preserve, and enjoy the natural beauty of the outdoors. . . . " Based in Seattle, Washington, the club is now the third-largest such organization in the United States, with 15,000 members and five branches throughout Washington State.

The Mountaineers sponsors both classes and year-round outdoor activities in the Pacific Northwest, which include hiking, mountain climbing, ski-touring, snowshoeing, bicycling, camping, kayaking and canoeing, nature study, sailing, and adventure travel. The club's conservation division supports environmental causes through educational activities, sponsoring legislation, and presenting informational programs. All club activities are led by skilled, experienced volunteers, who are dedicated to promoting safe and responsible enjoyment and preservation of the outdoors.

If you would like to participate in these organized outdoor activities or the club's programs, consider a membership in The Mountaineers. For information and an application, write or call The Mountaineers, Club Headquarters, 300 Third Avenue West, Seattle, WA 98119; 206-284-6310.

The Mountaineers Books, an active, nonprofit publishing program of the club, produces guidebooks, instructional texts, historical works, natural history guides, and works on environmental conservation. All books produced by The Mountaineers fulfill the club's mission.

Send or call for our catalog of more than 450 outdoor titles:

The Mountaineers Books
1001 SW Klickitat Way, Suite 201
Seattle, WA 98134
800-553-4453
mbooks@mountaineersbooks.org
www.mountaineersbooks.org

The Mountaineers Books is proud to be a corporate sponsor of Leave No Trace, whose mission is to promote and inspire responsible outdoor recreation through education, research, and partnerships. The Leave No Trace program is focused specifically on human-powered (non-motorized) recreation.

Leave No Trace strives to educate visitors about the nature of their recreational impacts, as well as offer techniques to prevent and minimize such impacts. Leave No Trace is best understood as an educational and ethical program, not as a set of rules and regulations.

For more information, visit *www.lnt.org*, or call 800-332-4100.

Available at fine bookstores and outdoor stores, by phone at (800) 553-4453, or on the Web at *www.mountaineersbooks.org*

EXPLORING WASHINGTON'S WILD AREAS: A Guide for Hikers, Backpackers, Climbers, Cross-Country Skiers, and Paddlers, 2nd Edition by Marge and Ted Mueller. $18.95 paperback. 0-89886-807-6.

100 CLASSIC HIKES IN™ WASHINGTON by Ira Spring and Harvey Manning. $19.95 paperback. 0-89886-586-7.

BEST OF THE PACIFIC CREST TRAIL: Washington: 55 Hikes by Dan Nelson. $16.95 paperback. 0-89886-703-7.

75 SCRAMBLES IN WASHINGTON: Classic Routes to the Summits by Peggy Goldman. $18.95 paperback. 0-89886-761-4.

HIKING WASHINGTON'S GEOLOGY by Scott Babcock and Robert Carson. $16.95 paperback. 0-89886-548-4.

100 CLASSIC BACKCOUNTRY SKI AND SNOWBOARD ROUTES IN WASHINGTON by Rainer Burgdorfer. $17.95 paperback. 0-89886-661-8.

SNOWSHOE ROUTES: Washington by Dan Nelson. $16.95 paperback. 0-89886-585-9.

WILDERNESS NAVIGATION: Finding Your Way Using Map, Compass, Altimeter, & GPS by Mike Burns and Bob Burns. $9.95 paperback. 0-89886-629-4.

GPS MADE EASY: Using Global Positioning Systems in the Outdoors, 3rd Edition by Lawrence Letham. $14.95 paperback. 0-89886-802-5.

FIRST AID: A Pocket Guide, 4th Edition by Christopher Van Tilburg, M.D. $3.50 paperback. 0-89886-719-3.

EMERGENCY SURVIVAL: A Pocket Guide by Christopher Van Tilburg, M.D. $3.50 paperback. 0-89886-768-1.

A FIELD GUIDE TO THE CASCADES & OLYMPICS by Stephen Whitney. $18.95 paperback. 0-89886-808-6